William McDonald

Beulah songs

A choice collection of popular hymns and music, new and old

William McDonald

Beulah songs

A choice collection of popular hymns and music, new and old

ISBN/EAN: 9783337264987

Printed in Europe, USA, Canada, Australia, Japan

Cover: Foto ©Thomas Meinert / pixelio.de

More available books at **www.hansebooks.com**

Beulah Songs.

A

CHOICE COLLECTION

OF

POPULAR HYMNS AND MUSIC,

NEW AND OLD.

ESPECIALLY ADAPTED TO CAMP MEETINGS, PRAYER AND CONFERENCE MEETINGS, FAMILY WORSHIP, AND ALL OTHER ASSEMBLIES WHERE JESUS IS PRAISED.

—BY—

Rev. W. McDONALD and Rev. L. HARTSOUGH.

NATIONAL
PUBLISHING ASSOCIATION FOR THE PROMOTION OF HOLINESS,
921 ARCH STREET, PHILADELPHIA.

J. S. Inskip, Agent.

Copyright, 1879, by Rev. W. McDonald and Rev. L. Hartsough.

PREFACE.

———o———

We have long felt the need of a cheap, well selected Collection of Words and Music adapted to Evangelistic work, especially to the higher forms of religious experience. This need has induced us to prepare this collection, which we commend to all the lovers of spiritual Christianity. In it will be found music, original and selected, which we are sure will make glad the hearts of the saints.

We take pleasure in expressing our obligations to W. G. Fischer, W. J. Kirkpatrick, Philip Phillips, Mrs. J. F. Knapp, W. W. Bentley, Rev. E. A. Hoffman, J. J. Hood, Mrs. J. H. Stockton, and several others, for valuable compositions which they have cheerfully contributed.

Beulah experiences are becoming more and more common, demanding "Beulah Songs" to give expression to such experiences.

> "*No storm can shake my inmost calm,*
> *While to this refuge clinging;*
> *While Christ is Lord of heaven and earth,*
> *How can I keep from singing.*"

W. McDONALD.
L. HARTSOUGH.

T. H. Lenfest, Music Typographer, School St. Boston.

BEULAH SONGS.

1. Bringing in the Sheaves.

"The harvest is the end of the world." —Matt. xiii: 39.

GEORGE A. MINOR.

1. Sowing in the morning, sowing seeds of kindness, Sowing in the noon-tide
2. Sowing in the sunshine, sowing in the shadows, Fearing neither clouds nor
3. Go, then, ev-er weeping, sowing for the Master, Tho' the loss sustain'd our

and the dew-y eve; Waiting for the harvest, and the time of reaping,
win-ter's chilling breeze; By-and-by the harvest, and the la-bor end-ed,
spir-it often grieves; When our weeping's o-ver, He will bid us welcome,

Chorus.

We shall come, re-joic-ing, Bringing in the sheaves. Bringing in the sheaves,
We shall come, re-joic-ing, Bringing in the sheaves. Bringing in the sheaves,
We shall come, re-joic-ing, Bringing in the sheaves. Bringing in the sheaves,

Bringing in the sheaves, We shall come, rejoicing, bringing in the sheaves. [sheaves.
Bringing in the sheaves, We shall come, rejoicing, (*omit.*) bringing in the

From "Golden Light," by permission.

2. I am Glad there is Cleansing.

Words and Music by Rev. L. HARTSOUGH.   Harmonized by ALICE L. HARTSOUGH.

1. How bright the Hope that Calv'ry brings, Where Love divine with Mercy blends;
2. 'Tis there! 'tis there the soul may go, And wash its sins and stains a-way;
3. Speak, speak to Zi-on's burden'd ones, Lead, lead them up to Calv'ry's Mount;
4. Why need we struggle on in self, We cannot make one black spot white;
5. I come! I come! and glad I am That Je-sus calls the lost and vile;

How full the joy that all may find, Where flows the Blood can save and cleanse.
Who gives up all,—who comes by faith, This cleansing finds without de-lay.
The want of aching hearts is met, 'Tis cleansing in Redemption's Fount.
'Tis Christ's own Blood, and that a-lone Can change and cleanse the heart aright.
There thousands have a cleansing found, I'll heed the Saviour's welcome smile.

I am glad there is cleansing in the Blood, I am glad there is

Chorus.
I am glad there is cleansing, there is cleansing in the Blood, I am glad there is cleansing in the Blood, Tell the world All the world, cleansing, there is cleansing in the Blood, Tell the world there is cleansing, All the world there is cleansing, There is cleansing in the Saviour's Blood.

Copyright, 1879, by Rev. L. HARTSOUGH.

3 I am Trusting, Lord, in Thee.

Words by Rev. WM. McDONALD. WM. G. FISCHER.

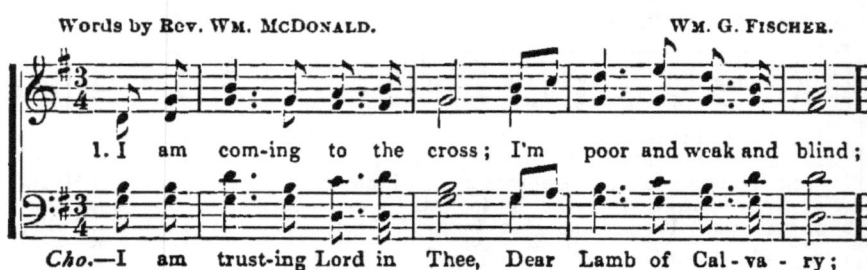

1. I am com-ing to the cross; I'm poor and weak and blind;

Cho.—I am trust-ing Lord in Thee, Dear Lamb of Cal-va-ry;

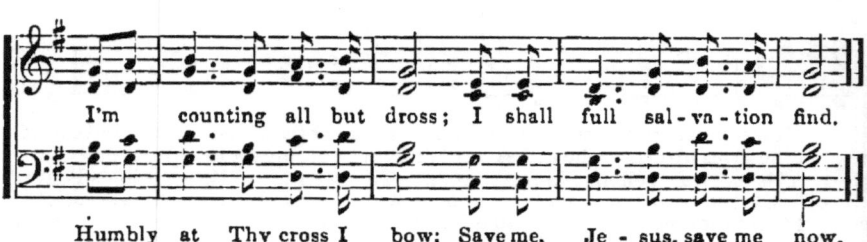

I'm counting all but dross; I shall full sal-va-tion find.

Humbly at Thy cross I bow; Save me, Je-sus, save me now.

2 Long my heart has sigh'd for thee;
Long has evil dwelt within;
Jesus sweetly speaks to me,
I will cleanse you from all sin.—*Cho.*

3 Here, I give my all to thee,—
Friends, and time, and earthly store,
Soul and body thine to be—
Wholly thine—forevermore.—*Cho.*

4 In the promises I trust;
In the cleansing blood confide;
I am prostrate in the dust;
I with Christ am crucified.—*Cho.*

5 Jesus comes! he fills my soul!
Perfected in love I am;
I am every whit made whole;
Glory, glory, to the Lamb!
(Chorus to 5th verse.)
Still I'm trusting, Lord, in Thee,
Dear Lamb of Calvary;
Humbly at Thy cross I bow—
Jesus saves me! saves me now.

---

4 PLENTEOUS GRACE IN JESUS.

1 Jesus, lover of my soul,
Let me to thy bosom fly,
While the nearer waters roll,
While the tempest still is high;
Hide me, O, my Saviour, hide,
Till the storm of life is past;
Safe into the haven guide,
O, receive my soul at last.

2 Other refuge have I none,
Hangs my helpless soul on thee,
Leave, O leave me not alone,
Still support and comfort me:
All my trust on thee is stayed,
All my help from thee I bring,
Cover my defenceless head
With the shadow of thy wing.

3 Thou, O Christ, art all I want;
More than all in thee I find;
Raise the fallen, cheer the faint,
Heal the sick, and lead the blind.
Just and holy is thy name;
I am all unrighteousness;
False and full of sin I am;
Thou art full of truth and grace.

4 Plenteous grace with thee is found,
Grace to cover all my sin,
Let the healing streams abound,
Make and keep me pure within.
Thou of life the fountain art,
Freely let me take of thee,
Spring thou up within my heart,
Rise to all eternity.

5 The Cleansing Wave.

(By Permission.)

Words by Mrs. PHOEBE PALMER.   Music by Mrs. J. F. KNAPP.

1. Oh, now I see the crimson wave, The fountain deep and wide, Jesus, my Lord, mighty to save, Points to His wounded side.

Chorus.
The cleansing stream, I see, I see! I plunge, and Oh, it cleanseth me! Oh, praise the Lord, it cleanseth me! It cleanseth me, yes, cleanseth me!

2 I see the new creation rise,
   I hear the speaking blood;
 It speaks! polluted nature dies!
   Sinks 'neath the cleansing flood.
     Chorus.—The cleansing stream, &c.

3 I rise to walk in heaven's own light,
   Above the world and sin,
 With heart made pure, and garments white,
   And Christ enthroned within.
     Chorus.—The cleansing stream, &c.

4 Amazing grace! 'tis heaven below,
   To feel the blood applied;
 And Jesus, only Jesus know,
   My Jesus crucified.
     Chorus.—The cleansing stream, &c.

6   *The blood of sprinkling.*   C. M.

1 My God, my God, to Thee I cry;
   Thee only would I know;
  Thy purifying blood apply,
   And wash me white as snow.
2 Touch me, and make the leper clean;
   Purge my iniquity:
  Unless Thou wash my soul from sin,
   I have no part in Thee.
3 But art Thou not already mine?
   Answer, if mine Thou art;
  Whisper within, Thou love divine,
   And cheer my drooping heart.
4 Behold, for me the Victim bleeds,—
   His wounds are open wide;
  For me the blood of sprinkling pleads,
   And speaks me justified.

7   *For the waters of salvation.*   C. M.

1 Fountain of life, to all below
   Let Thy salvation roll;
  Water, replenish, and o'erflow
   Every believing soul.
2 Into that happy number, Lord,
   Us weary sinners take;
  Jesus, fulfil Thy gracious word,
   For Thine own mercy's sake.
3 Turn back our nature's rapid tide,
   And we shall flow to Thee,
  While down the stream of time we glide
   To our eternity.
4 The Well of life to us Thou art,—
   Of joy, the swelling flood:
  Wafted by Thee, with willing heart,
   We swift return to God.
5 We soon shall reach the boundless sea;
   Into Thy fulness fall;
  Be lost and swallow'd up in Thee,—
   Our God, our All in All.

8   *Determined importunity.*   C. M.

1 Because for me the Saviour prays,
   And pleads His death for me,
  God hath vouchsafed a longer space,
   And spared the barren tree.
2 I now from all my sins would turn
   To my atoning God;
  And look on Him I pierced, and mourn,
   And feel the sprinkled blood:—
3 Would nail my passions to the cross,
   Where my Redeemer died;
  And all things else account but loss
   For Jesus crucified.
4 Giver of penitential pain,
   Before Thy cross I lie;
  In grief determined to remain
   Till Thou Thy blood apply.

5 Forgiveness on my conscience seal;
   Bestow Thy promised rest:
  With purest love Thy servant fill,
   And number with the blest.

9   *Blessedness of adoption.*   C. M.

1 And can my heart aspire so high
   To say—My Father, God?
  Lord, at Thy feet I fain would lie,
   And learn to kiss the rod.
2 I would submit to all Thy will,
   For Thou art good and wise;
  Let each rebellious thought be still,
   Nor one faint murmur rise.
3 Thy love can cheer the darkest gloom,
   And bid me wait serene,
  Till hopes and joys immortal bloom,
   And brighten all the scene.
4 My Father, God, permit my heart
   To plead her humble claim,
  And ask the bliss those words impart,
   In my Redeemer's name.

10   *I would be Thine.*   C. M.

1 I would be Thine; O take my heart,
   And fill it with Thy love;
  Thy sacred image, Lord, impart,
   And seal it from above.
2 I would be Thine; but while I strive
   To give myself away,
  I feel rebellion still alive,
   And wander while I pray.
3 I would be Thine; but, Lord, I feel
   Evil still lurks within:—
  Do Thou Thy majesty reveal,
   And overcome my sin.
4 I would be Thine; I would embrace
   The Saviour, and adore;
  Inspire with faith, infuse thy grace,
   And now my soul restore.

11   *Peace in believing.*   C. M.

1 Jesus, to Thee I now can fly,
   On whom my help is laid:
  Oppress'd by sins, I lift mine eye,
   And see the shadows fade.
2 Believing on my Lord, I find
   A sure and present aid:
  On Thee alone my constant mind
   Be every moment stay'd.
3 Whate'er in me seems wise, or good,
   Or strong, I here disclaim:
  I wash my garments in the blood
   Of the atoning Lamb.
4 Jesus, my strength, my life, my rest,—
   On Thee will I depend,
  Till summon'd to the marriage-feast,
   When faith in sight shall end.

12. Deliverance will Come.

Arr. by Rev. W. McDonald.

1. I saw a way-worn trav'ler
   In tattered garments clad,
   His back was laden heavy,
   His strength was almost gone,
   And struggling up the mountain,
   It seem'd that he was sad;
   Yet he shouted as he journeyed,
   Deliverance will come.

   Chorus.
   Then palms of victory,
   Crowns of glory,
   Palms of victory,
   I shall bear.

2. The summer sun was shining,
   The sweat was on his brow,
   His garments worn and dusty,
   His step seemed very slow:
   But he kept pressing onward,
   For he was wending home;
   Still shouting as he journeyed,
   Deliverance will come.
   Chorus.—Then palms, &c.

3. The songsters in the arbor
   That grew beside the way,
   Attracted his attention,
   Inviting his delay:
   His watchword being 'Onward'
   He stopped his ears and ran,
   Still shouting as he journeyed,
   Deliverance will come.—*Chorus.*

4. I saw him in the evening,
   The sun was bending low,
   Had overtopped the mountain
   And reached the vale below:
   He saw the golden city,
   His everlasting home,
   And shouted loud hosannah!
   Deliverance will come.—*Chorus.*

5. While gazing on that city
   Just o'er the narrow flood,
   A band of holy angels
   Came from the throne of God:
   They bore him on their pinions,
   Safe o'er the dashing foam,
   And joined him in his triumph,—
   Deliverance has come.—*Chorus.*

6. I heard the song of triumph
   They sang upon that shore,
   Saying, Jesus has redeemed us,
   To suffer nevermore:
   Then casting his eyes backward,
   On the race which he had ran,
   He shouted loud hosanna!
   Deliverance has come.—*Chorus.*

Copyright, 1876, by Rev. W. McDonald.

13 Who'll stand up for Jesus?

By per. of PHILIP PHILLIPS.   Words and Music by Rev. L. HARTSOUG.

1. O, who'll stand up for Jesus, The lowly Nazarene?
And raise the blood-stain'd banner Amid the hosts of sin?

Chorus.

The cross for Christ I'll cherish, Its crucifixion bear;
All hail! reproach or sorrow, If Jesus leads me there.

2 O, who will follow Jesus,
   Amid reproach and shame?
Where others shrink or falter,
   Who'll glory in His Name?
    Chorus.

3 Though fierce may rage the battle,
   And wild the storm may blow,—
Though friends may go forever,
   Who will with Jesus go?
    Chorus.

4 My all to Christ I've given,
   My talents, time, and voice,
Myself, my reputation,
   The lone way is my choice.
    Chorus.

5 O Jesus, Jesus, Jesus,
   My all-sufficient Friend!
Come, fold me to Thy bosom,
   E'en to the journey's end.
    Chorus.

14. Consecration.

From "*Notes of Joy*," by Mrs. JOSEPH H. KNAPP. Words by MARY D. JAMES. By Permission.
Written at the National Camp Meeting, Round Lake, July 10, 1869.

1. My body, soul and spirit, Jesus, I give to Thee,

A consecrated offering, Thine evermore to be.

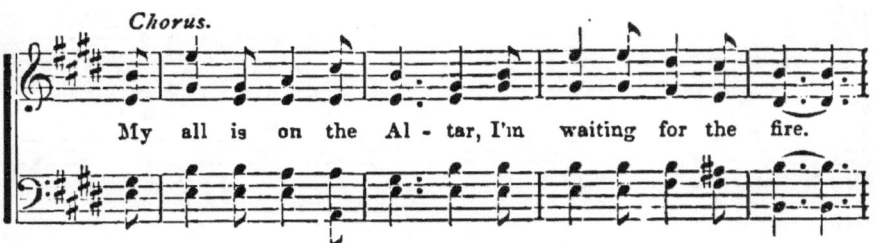

Chorus.
My all is on the Altar, I'm waiting for the fire.

ritard.
Waiting, waiting, waiting, I'm waiting for the fire.

2
O Jesus, mighty Saviour,
  I trust in Thy great name,
I look for Thy salvation,
  Thy promise now I claim.

Chorus.—My all is on the Altar,
  I'm waiting for the fire,
Waiting, waiting, waiting,
  I'm waiting for the fire.

3
O let the fire, descending
  Just now upon my soul,
Consume my humble offering,
  And cleanse and make me whole.

4
I'm Thine, O blessed Jesus,
  Wash'd by Thy cleansing blood,
Now seal me by Thy Spirit
  A sacrifice to God.

2
Close to Thee, when weak and faint,
Duty's path pursuing,
Let me feel Thy circling arm,
All my strength renewing.

3
Close to Thee, O Lamb of God,
Near Thy cross abiding;
I can brave the tempest shower,
In Thy love confiding.

4
Close to Thee, when earthly ties,
One by one are breaking;
When my soul to life anew,
Glad and pure is waking.

5
Close to Thee amid the throng,
By life's crystal river;
Close to Thee shall be my song
In the bright forever.

16 Beulah Land.

EDGAR PAGE.
"He shall give thee the desires of thine heart."
JNO. R. SWENEY.

1. I've reach'd the land of corn and wine, And all its rich-es free-ly mine,
Here shines undimm'd one blissful day, For all my night has pass'd a-way.

2. My Saviour comes and walks with me, And sweet communion here have we;
He gent-ly leads me by his hand, For this is heaven's bor-der-land.

3. A sweet perfume up-on the breeze, Is borne from ev-er ver-nal trees,
And flow'rs, that never fading grow Where streams of life for-ev-er flow.

4. The zephyrs seem to float to me Sweet sounds of heaven's mel-o-dy,
As angels with the white-rob'd throng Join in the sweet re-demption song.

Chorus.

O Beulah Land, sweet Beulah Land, As on thy high-est mount I stand,
I look a-way a-cross the sea, Where mansions are prepared for me,
And view the shining glo-ry shore, My heav'n, my home, for ev-er-more!

From "Garner," by permission of Publisher.

17 Cleansing Fountain. C. M.

COWPER. Arranged by Rev. L. H.

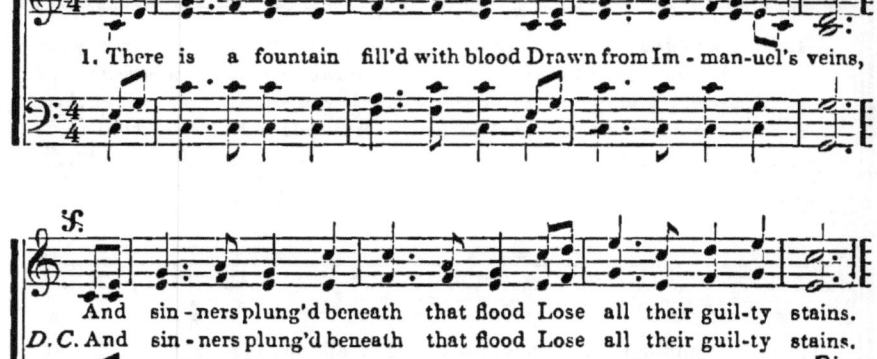

2 The dying thief rejoiced to see
   That fountain in his day;
   And there have I, as vile as he,
   Wash'd all my sins away.

3 Dear dying Lamb, thy precious blood
   Shall never lose its power,
   Till all the ransom'd Church of God
   Be saved, to sin no more.

4 E'er since by faith I saw the stream
   Thy flowing wounds supply,
   Redeeming love has been my theme,
   And shall be till I die.

5 Then in a nobler, sweeter song,
   I'll sing thy power to save,
   When this poor lisping, stam'ring tongue
   Lies silent in the grave.

18 LONGING TO BE DISSOLVED IN LOVE.

1 Jesus hath died that I might live,
   Might live to God alone;
   In him eternal life receive,
   And be in spirit one.

2 Saviour, I thank thee for the grace,
   The gift unspeakable:
   And wait with arms of faith t' embrace,
   And all thy love to feel.

3 My soul breaks out in strong desire
   The perfect bliss to prove;
   My longing heart is all on fire
   To be dissolved in love.

4 Give me thyself: from every boast,
   From every wish set free;
   Let all I am in thee be lost,
   But give thyself to me.

5 Thy gifts, alas! cannot suffice,
   Unless thyself be given;
   Thy presence makes my paradise,
   And where thou art is heaven.

19. Rejoice and be Glad.

Rev. Horatius Bonar, 1874.   *English Melody.*

1. Re-joice and be glad! The Redeemer has come! Go look on His cradle, His cross, and His tomb. Sound His prais-es, tell the Sto-ry, Of Him who was slain; Sound His praises, tell with gladness, He liv-eth a-gain.

last of Cho. to 7th verse.—He com-eth a-gain.

2 Rejoice and be glad!
  It is sunshine at last!
  The clouds have departed,
  The shadows are past.—*Chorus.*

3 Rejoice and be glad!
  For the blood hath been shed;
  Redemption is finished,
  The price hath been paid.—*Chorus.*

4 Rejoice and be glad!
  Now the pardon is free!
  The Just for the unjust
  Hath died on the tree.—*Chorus.*

5 Rejoice and be glad!
  For the Lamb that was slain,
  O'er death is triumphant,
  And liveth again.—*Chorus.*

6 Rejoice and be glad!
  For our King is on high,
  He pleadeth for us on
  His throne in the sky.—*Chorus.*

7 Rejoice and be glad!
  For He cometh again;
  He cometh in glory,
  The Lamb that was slain.—*Chorus.*

---

20 REVIVE US AGAIN.

1 We praise Thee, O God! for the Son of Thy love,
  For Jesus who died, and is now gone above.

Chorus.—Hallelujah! Thine the glory, Hallelujah! Amen,
  Hallelujah! Thine the glory, revive us again.

2 All glory and praise to the Lamb that was slain,
  Who has borne all our sins, and cleansed every stain.—*Chorus.*

3 All glory and praise to the God of all grace,
  Who has bought us, and sought us, and guided our ways.—*Chorus.*

4 Revive us again; fill each heart with Thy love,
  May each soul be kindled with fire from above.—*Chorus.*

Rev. Wm. Paton Mackey, 1866.

21. I hear Thy welcome Voice.

From "Song Sermons," by per. of PHILIP PHILLIPS.
Words and Music by Rev. L. HARTSOUGH.

1. I hear Thy welcome voice, That calls me Lord to Thee;
For cleansing in Thy precious Blood, That flow'd on Cal-va-ry.

2. Tho' coming weak and vile, Thou dost my strength as-sure;
Thou dost my vile-ness ful-ly cleanse, Till spotless all, and pure.

Chorus.
I am coming, Lord! Coming now to Thee!
Wash me, cleanse me, in the Blood That flow'd on Cal-va-ry.

3
'Tis Jesus calls me on
To Perfect Faith and Love,
To Perfect Hope, and Peace, and Trust,
For Earth and Heaven above.
Chorus.—I am coming, &c.

4
'Tis Jesus who confirms,
The blessed work within,
By adding grace, to welcomed grace,
Where reigned the power of sin.
Chorus.—I am coming, &c.

5
And he the witness gives
To loyal hearts and free,
That every promise is fulfilled,
If faith but brings the plea.
Chorus.—I am coming, &c.

6
All hail! atoning blood!
All hail! redeeming grace!
All hail! the gift of Christ, our Lord,
Our strength and righteousness.
Chorus.—I am coming, &c.

22. White as Snow.

Words by Rev. W. McDonald. Arr. by Rev. W. McD.

1. Ah, many years my burden'd heart Has sighed, has long'd to know
The virtue of my Saviour's blood, That washes white as snow.

2. I heard the saints in rapture tell, How much a soul may know
Of Jesus' precious cleansing blood, That washes white as snow.

Chorus.
There is pow'r in Jesus' blood, There is pow'r in Jesus' blood, There is pow'r in Jesus' blood To wash me white as snow.

3
I came to Jesus sick and vile,
 That I this grace might know;
And trusted in his precious blood
 To wash me white as snow.—*Cho.*

4
He cast on me a look of love,
 Such as no words can show;
I felt within my very soul
 He wash'd me white as snow.—*Cho.*

5
I'll tell to every saint I meet,
 To sinners high and low,
That, trusting in the Saviour's blood,
 It washes white as snow.—*Cho.*

6
And when to that bright world above,
 My raptur'd soul shall go,
My song shall be—The precious blood,
 Still washes white as snow.—*Cho.*

Copyright, 1879, by Rev. W. McDonald.

23. Child, your Father calls.

(Dedicated to Chaplain McCabe.)

ANNIE M. STOCKTON.   Music by Rev. J. H. STOCKTON. by per.

1. Come home, dear sinner, while the light Is beaming on your way,—
The door stands open wide for you, Return while yet you may.

Chorus.
Come home, come home, dear child, come home, Your Father bids you come;
Come home, come home, just now come home, O weary wand'rer come.

2
Come home, dear sinner; by the cross,
  Your Saviour waits for you;
He'll cleanse away your earthly dross,
  And make you happy too.—*Cho.*

3
Come home, dear sinner, while you feel
  The spirit move your heart;
While at the mercy-seat you kneel,
  With every idol part.—*Cho.*

4
Come home, dear sinner, while you may,
  The church is calling, too:
With earnest faith begin to pray,
  And heav'n will welcome you.—*Cho.*

5
Come home, dear sinner, Jesus' blood
  Can wash out every stain;
Plunge now into the crimson flood
  Of him who once was slain.—*Cho.*

Copyright, 1875, by Rev. J. H. STOCKTON.

24 Companionship with Jesus.

Words by Mrs. MARY D. JAMES.   Music by W. J. KIRKPATRICK. by per.

1. Oh, blessed fellowship divine! Oh, joy supremely sweet! Companionship with

Je-sus here, Makes life with bliss replete. In union with the purest one I

Chorus.
find my heav'n on earth begun. Oh, wondrous bliss, oh, joy sublime, I've Jesus with me

all the time. Oh, wondrous bliss, oh, joy sublime, I've Jesus with me all the time.

2
I'm walking close to Jesus' side,—
  So close that I can hear
The softest whispers of his love,—
  In fellowship so dear,
And feel his great Almighty hand
Protects me in this hostile land.—*Cho.*

3
I'm leaning on his loving breast,
  Along life's weary way;
My path, illumined by his smiles,
  Grows brighter day by day.
No foes, no woes my heart can fear,
With my Almighty Friend so near.—*Cho.*

4
I know his shelt'ring wings of love
  Are always o'er me spread,
And tho' the storms may fiercely rage,
  All calm and free from dread,
My peaceful spirit ever sings
"I'll trust the covert of thy wings."

25 I cling, Dear Lord, to Thee.

Words and Melody by Rev. L. HARTSOUGH. Arranged by ALICE HARTSOUGH.

2 I cling, dear Lord, to Thee,
  In trials all severe;
Temptations close me so around,
  With much of care and fear.
      Chorus.

3 I cling, dear Lord, to Thee,
  From sin to find a cure;
From condemnation set me free,
  From all that may allure.
      Chorus.

4 I cling, dear Lord, to Thee;
  I feel so safe and strong
When in Thy smiles I may abide,
  Though foes around me throng.
      Chorus.

5 I cling, I cling to Thee
  For pow'r to love Thee well,
To serve Thee with a purer heart,
  Thy praises oft to tell.
      Chorus.

Copyright, 1878, *by Rev. L. HARTSOUGH.*

26. Whiter than Snow.

JAMES NICHOLSON.   WM. G. FISCHER, by per.

1. Dear Jesus, I long to be perfectly whole; I want Thee forever, to live in my soul; Break down ev-'ry idol, cast out every foe; Now, wash me, and I shall be whiter than snow.

Chorus.—Whiter than snow, yes, whiter than snow; Now wash me and I shall be whiter than snow.

2. Dear Jesus, let nothing unholy remain, Apply thine own blood, and remove ev-'ry stain. To have this blest cleansing I all things forego; Now wash me, &c.

last of Cho. to 6th verse.—Dear Jesus, thy blood makes me whiter than snow.

3 Dear Jesus, come down from thy throne in the skies,
And help me to make a complete sacrifice.
I give up myself, and whatever I know—
Now wash me, and I shall be whiter than snow.—*Chorus.*

4 Dear Jesus, thou seest I patiently wait,
Come now, and within me a clean heart create,
To those who have sought thee thou never saidst no,
Now wash me, and I shall be whiter than snow.—*Chorus.*

5 Dear Jesus, for this I most humbly entreat;
I wait, blessed Lord, at thy crucified feet,
By faith, for my cleansing, I see thy blood flow—
Now wash me, and I shall be whiter than snow.—*Chorus.*

6 The blessing by faith, I receive from above;
O glory! my soul is made perfect in love;
My prayer has prevailed, and this moment I know,
The blood is applied, I am whiter than snow.—*Chorus.*

Jesus, my Joy.

Words by Mrs. J. F. CREWDSON. Music by W. J. KIRKPATRICK, by per.

1. I've found a joy in sorrow, A secret balm for pain,
A beautiful tomorrow Of sunshine after rain.

2. I've found a branch for healing, Near ev'ry bitter spring,
A whisper'd promise stealing O'er ev'ry broken string.

Chorus.
'Tis Jesus, my portion forever, 'Tis Jesus, the First and the Last;
A help very present in trouble, A shelter from ev'ry blast.

3
I've found a glad hosanna
For every woe and wail,
A handful of sweet manna,
When grapes of Eschol fail.—*Cho.*

4
I've found the Rock of Ages,
When desert wells are dry;
And after weary stages,
I've found an Elim nigh.—*Cho.*

5
An Elim with its coolness,
Its fountains and its shade;
A blessing in its fulness,
When buds of promise fade.—*Cho.*

6
O'er tears of soft contrition
I've seen a rainbow light:
A glory and fruition,
So near! yet out of sight.—*Cho.*

Copyright, 1875, by W. J. KIRKPATRICK.

28. Take me as I am.

Melody by the late Rev. J. H. STOCKTON. Har. by W. J. K.

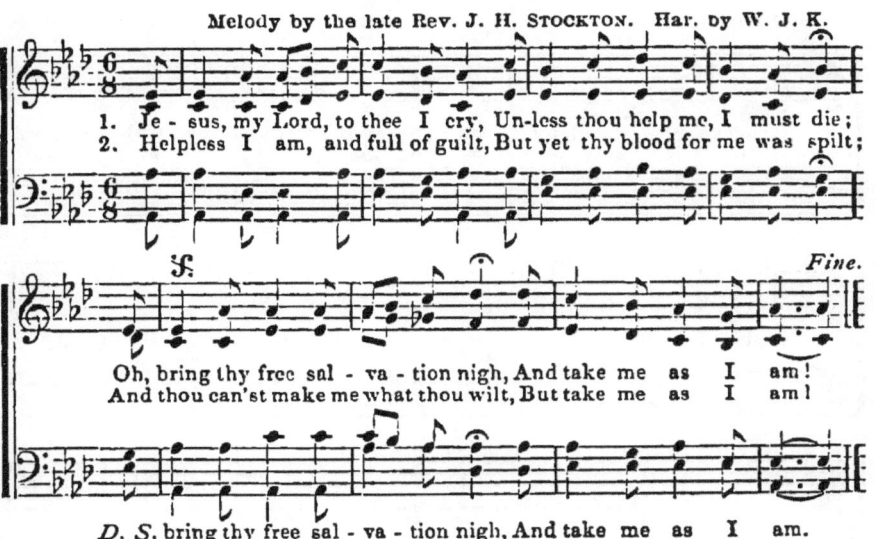

1. Je-sus, my Lord, to thee I cry, Un-less thou help me, I must die;
Oh, bring thy free sal-va-tion nigh, And take me as I am!
2. Helpless I am, and full of guilt, But yet thy blood for me was spilt;
And thou can'st make me what thou wilt, But take me as I am!

D. S. bring thy free sal-va-tion nigh, And take me as I am.

Refrain.

Take me as I am,.... Take me as I am; Oh,

3 No preparation can I make,
My best resolves I only break;
Yet save me for thine own name's sake,
And take me as I am!

4 I thirst, I long to know thy love,
Thy full salvation I would prove;
But since to thee I cannot move,
Oh, take me as I am!

5 If thou hast work for me to do,
Inspire my will, my heart renew,
And work both in and by me too,
But take me as I am!

6 And when at last the work is done,
The battle o'er, the vict'ry won,
Still, still my cry shall be alone,
Lord, take me as I am!

JUST AS I AM.—Tune and Chorus above.

1 Just as I am, without one plea,
But that thy blood was shed for me,
And that thou bid'st me come to thee,
O, Lamb of God, I come!

2 Just as I am, and waiting not
To rid my soul of one dark blot, [spot,
To thee, whose blood can cleanse each
O, Lamb of God, I come!

3 Just as I am, though tossed about
With many a conflict, many a doubt;
Fightings within, and fears without,
O, Lamb of God, I come!

4 Just as I am, poor, wretched, blind,
Sight, riches, healing of the mind,
Yea, all I need in thee to find,
O, Lamb of God, I come!

5 Just as I am, thou wilt receive,
Wilt welcome, pardon, cleanse, relieve;
Because thy promise I believe,
O, Lamb of God, I come!

6 Just as I am, thy love unknown
Hath broken every barrier down;
Now, to be thine, and thine alone,
O, Lamb of God, I come!

29. Come to Jesus.

By Permission. Words and Music by Rev. J. H. STOCKTON.

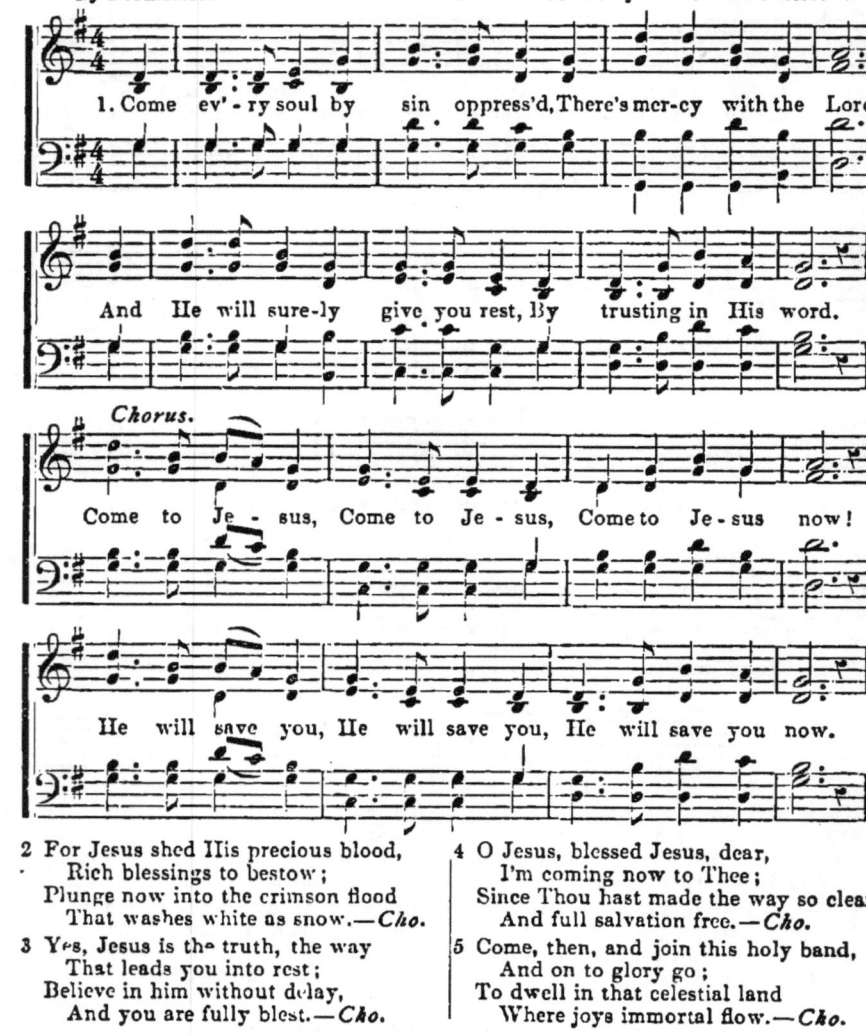

1. Come ev'ry soul by sin oppress'd, There's mercy with the Lord: And He will surely give you rest, By trusting in His word.

Chorus.
Come to Jesus, Come to Jesus, Come to Jesus now! He will save you, He will save you, He will save you now.

2 For Jesus shed His precious blood,
  Rich blessings to bestow;
Plunge now into the crimson flood
  That washes white as snow.—*Cho.*

3 Yes, Jesus is the truth, the way
  That leads you into rest;
Believe in him without delay,
  And you are fully blest.—*Cho.*

4 O Jesus, blessed Jesus, dear,
  I'm coming now to Thee;
Since Thou hast made the way so clear,
  And full salvation free.—*Cho.*

5 Come, then, and join this holy band,
  And on to glory go;
To dwell in that celestial land
  Where joys immortal flow.—*Cho.*

30. DEDICATION TO THE LORD. C. Wesley.

1 Let Him to whom we now belong,
  His sov'reign right assert;
And take up every thankful song,
  And every loving heart.
Cho.—Here with Jesus, here with Jesus,
  Only Jesus now:
For He saves us, sweetly saves us,
  Jesus saves us now.

2 He justly claims us for His own,
  Who bought us with a price;
The Christian lives to Christ alone;
  To Christ alone he dies.—*Cho.*

3 Jesus, Thine own at last receive:
  Fulfil our hearts' desire;
And let us to thy glory live,
  And in Thy cause expire.—*Cho.*

4 Our souls and bodies we resign;
  With joy we render Thee
Our all,—no longer ours, but Thine
  To all eternity.—*Chorus.*

31. I'm Redeemed.

Words by Rev. W. McDonald. Arr. by Rev. W. McDonald.

1. Jesus, Lord, I come to Thee, Wash'd in the blood of the Lamb!
Set my longing spirit free, Wash'd in the blood of the Lamb!

Chorus.
I'm redeem'd, redeem'd, Wash'd in the blood of the Lamb!
I'm redeem'd, redeem'd, I am wash'd in the blood of the Lamb!

2 Speak, and let my heart be clean, Wash'd, etc.
Fully sav'd from inbred sin, Wash'd, etc.
Chorus.—I'm redeem'd, redeem'd, etc.

3 Cleanse me, wash me white as snow, Wash'd, etc.
Let me all Thy fullness know, Wash'd, etc.
Chorus.—I'm redeem'd, redeem'd, etc.

4 To my heart the bliss reveal, Wash'd, etc.
Fix on me the Spirit's seal, Wash'd, etc.
Chorus.—I'm redeem'd, redeem'd, etc.

5 All thy fullness now I claim, Wash'd, etc.
Through the dear Redeemer's name, Wash'd, etc.
Chorus.—I'm redeem'd, redeem'd, etc.

6 I am sav'd by blood divine, Wash'd, etc.
All the bliss of faith is mine, Wash'd, etc.
Chorus.—I'm redeem'd, redeem'd, etc.

32. I Rest Upon His Promise.

CHARLES WESLEY. R. E. HUDSON, by per.

1. Lord, I believe a rest remains To all thy people known;
   A rest where pure enjoyment reigns, And Thou art lov'd alone.
2. A rest, where all our soul's desire Is fix'd on things above;
   Where fear, and sin and grief expire, Cast out by perfect love.
3. Oh! that I now the rest might know, Believe, and enter in;
   Now, Saviour, now the pow'r bestow, And let me cease from sin.
4. Remove this hardness from my heart; This unbelief, remove;
   To me the rest of faith impart—The Sabbath of Thy love.

CHORUS.

I rest upon His promise, sure; I come, I wait, to prove
The cleansing of my heart from sin, The fullness of His love.

From " Gems of Gospel Songs," published by R. E. Hudson, Alliance, O.

33. Full Salvation.

Words by LOUISE M. ROUSE. Music by Miss DORA BOOLE.

1. Precious Saviour, thou hast sav'd me: Thine and on-ly thine I am: Oh! the cleansing blood has reach'd me, Glo-ry, glo-ry to the Lamb!

Chorus.
Glo-ry, glo-ry, Je-sus saves me, Glo-ry, glo-ry to the Lamb! Oh! the cleansing blood has reach'd me, Glo-ry, glo-ry to the Lamb.

2 Long my yearning heart was trying
   To enjoy this perfect rest;
But I gave all trying over:
   Simply trusting, I was blest.—*Cho.*

3 Trusting, trusting every moment;
   Feeling now the blood applied;
Lying at the cleansing fountain;
   Dwelling in my Saviour's side.—*Cho.*

4 Consecrated to thy service,
   I will live and die to thee:
I will witness to thy glory
   Of salvation full and free.—*Cho.*

5 Yes, I will stand up for Jesus;
   He has sweetly saved my soul,
Cleansed me from inbred corruption,
   Sanctified, and made me whole.—*Cho.*

6 Glory to the blood that bought me,
   Glory to its cleansing power!
Glory to the blood that keeps me!
   Glory, glory, evermore!—*Cho.*

34. Wondrous Love.

Mrs. M. Stockton.   Wm. G. Fischer, by per.

1. God lov'd the world of sinners lost, And ruin'd by the fall; Salvation full at highest cost, He offers free to all.

Chorus.
O, 'twas love, 'twas wondrous love! The love of God to me, It brought my Saviour from above, To die on Calvary.

2
E'en now by faith I claim Him mine,
  The risen Son of God;
Redemption by his death I find,
  And cleansing through His blood.
                Chorus.

3
Love brings the glorious fullness in,
  And to his saints makes known,
The blessed rest from inbred sin,
  Through faith in Christ alone.
                Chorus.

4
Believing souls rejoicing go,
  There shall to you be given,
A glorious foretaste here below
  Of endless life in heaven.
                Chorus.

5
Of victory now o'er Satan's power,
  Let all the ransom'd sing
And triumph in the dying hour,
  Thro' Christ, the Lord, our King.
                Chorus.

35. The Great Physician.

Arranged by Rev. J. H. STOCKTON.   Har. for this Work.

1. The great Phy-si-cian now is near, The sym-pa-thiz-ing Je-sus,
He speaks the drooping heart to cheer, Oh, hear the voice of Je-sus.

Chorus.
Sweetest note in seraph song, Sweetest name on mortal tongue,
Sweet-est car-ol ev-er sung, Je-sus, Je-sus, Je-sus.

2
Your many sins are all forgiven,
  Oh! hear the voice of Jesus:
Go on your way in peace to heaven,
  And wear a crown with Jesus.
    Chorus.—Sweetest note, &c.

3
All glory to the dying Lamb,
  I now believe in Jesus:
I love the blessed Saviour's name,
  I love the name of Jesus.
    Chorus.—Sweetest note, &c.

4
His name dispels my guilt and fear,
  No other name but Jesus:
Oh! how my soul delights to hear
  The charming name of Jesus.
    Chorus.—Sweetest note, &c.

5
And when to that bright world above
  We rise to see our Jesus,
We'll sing around the throne of love,
  The name, the name of Jesus.
    Chorus.—Sweetest note, &c.

Copyright, 1872, by Rev. *J. H. STOCKTON.*

Entire Consecration.

Words by FRANCES RIDLEY HAVERGAL. Music by W. J. KIRKPATRICK, by per.

1. Take my life, and let it be Con-se-cra-ted, Lord to thee.
Take my hands and let them move At the im-pulse of thy love.

Chorus.
Wash me in the Saviour's precious blood,
Cleanse me in its pu-ri-fy-ing flood,
Lord I give to thee my life and all, to be Thine, hence-forth e-ter-nal-ly.

2
Take my feet, and let them be
Swift and beautiful for thee;
Take my voice, and let me sing
Always, only for my King.—*Chorus.*

3
Take my lips and let them be
Fill'd with messages from thee;
Take my moments and my days,
Let them flow in ceaseless praise.—*Cho.*

4
Take my will and make it thine;
It shall be no longer mine;
Take my heart—it is thine own,
It shall be thy royal throne.—*Chorus.*

5
Take my love—my Lord, I pour
At thy feet its treasure-store !
Take myself, and I will be
Ever, only, all for thee !—*Chorus.*

Copyright, 1875, by Rev. J. H. STOCKTON and W. J. KIRKPATRICK.

37 Are you Wash'd in the Blood?

Words and Music by Rev. Elisha A. Hoffman.

From "*Spiritual Songs*," by permission.

38 How Can I keep from Singing?

F. J. HARTLEY.
Rev. R. LOWRY.
From "Bright Jewels," by per.

1. My life flows on in end-less song; A-bove earth's lam-en-ta-tion,
I catch the sweet, tho' far-off hymn That hails a new cre-a-tion;
Through all the tu-mult and the strife, I hear the mu-sic ring-ing;
It finds an ech-o in my soul—How can I keep from sing-ing?

2
What though my joys and comfort die?
  The Lord, my Saviour, liveth;
What though the darkness gather round?
  Songs in the night he giveth:
No storm can shake my inmost calm,
  While to that refuge clinging:
Since Christ is Lord of heav'n and earth,
  How can I keep from singing?

3
I lift my eyes; the cloud grows thin;
  I see the blue above it;
And day by day this pathway smooths,
  Since first I learned to love it:
The peace of Christ makes fresh my heart,
  A fountain ever springing;
All things are mine since I am his—
  How can I keep from singing?

Copyright, 1869, by BIGLOW & MAIN.

39. Jesus Calls Me.

By per. of PHILIP PHILLIPS.   Words and Music by Rev. L. HARTSOUGH.

1. Jesus calls me; I am going
Where He opens up my way,
To the toiling of His vineyard,
Shrinking not a single day.
But I've chosen Christ my Saviour,
I am going, call me not.
Friends may shun me, toils await me,
Crucifixion be my lot;

2
Jesus calls me, I am going
To the life he wills for me;
This poor world can't fill the aching
Of my heart, or set it free.
O, what anxious, bitter sorrow
Does the world give with its strife;
But with Jesus,—O what glory!
Ending in eternal life.

3
Jesus calls me; I am going
To the washing of his blood,—
Healing now, and purifying
All who test the crimson flood;
Flesh may cry, not now,—to-morrow,—
Idols rise with wonted power;
Jesus, help me, come and help me!
Jesus take me hour by hour.

4
Jesus calls me; I am going
To the mansions all prepared,
These for thee, for all, says Jesus,
Who my pow'r hath here declar'd:
Knowing this complete Salvation,—
This that saves from inbred sin,
Why not tell to all around me,
Jesus can make wholly clean?

5
Jesus calls me; I am going;—
O that all would test with me,
All the power of Christ's Salvation,
For the fountain's full and free.
Test the grace so freely offered,
Know the worth of Christ within;
Rise and share the bliss transcendent—
Freedom from the power of sin.

40. Work for Jesus.

Rev. E. H. STOKES. WM. G. FISCHER, by per.

Dedicated to Preacher's Class of 1844, N. J. Conference.

1. We have toil'd in many vineyards, We have toil'd thro' many a day,
Toil'd for thee, O blessed Jesus, Worn for thee our strength away.

Chorus.
And we still will work for Jesus, Work for him has bless-ed pay:
We will ever work for Jesus, Work for him our lives away.

2
We have toil'd thro' storm and sunshine,
 Summer's heat, and winter's cold;
Toil is sweet in youth's bright morning,
 Sweet when men are growing old.
  Chorus.—And we still, &c.

3
We have toil'd in human gardens,
 Digging, sowing, pruning, too,
Praying for the dew and sunshine,
 On the work we found to do.
  Chorus.—And we still, &c.

4
Lo! the garden blooms with flowers,
 Fragrance fills the blessed air;
Living, dying, precious brethren,
 Toil for Jesus everywhere.
  Chorus.—Yes! we still, &c.

Copyright, 1874, by Wm. G. FISCHER.

41 Oh, Sing of His Mighty Love.

Words by Rev. F. BOTTOME, D. D.　　Music by WM. B. BRADBURY.

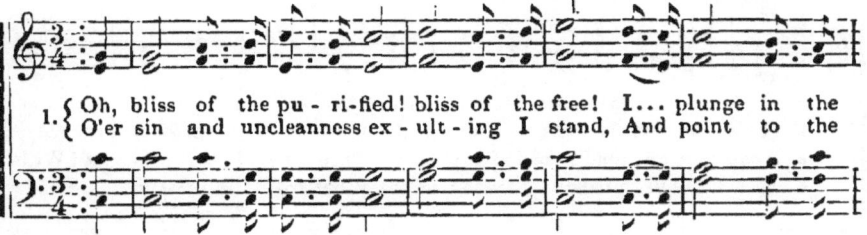

1. Oh, bliss of the pu-ri-fied! bliss of the free! I... plunge in the
   O'er sin and uncleanness ex-ult-ing I stand, And point to the

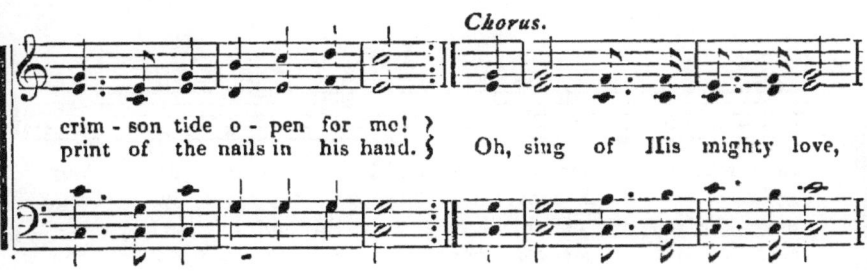

crim-son tide o-pen for me!
print of the nails in his hand.

Chorus. Oh, sing of His mighty love,

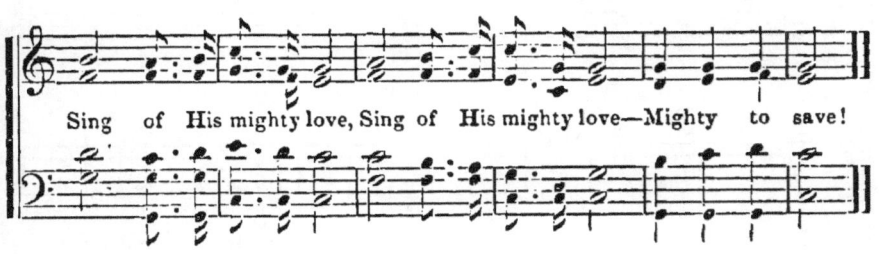

Sing of His mighty love, Sing of His mighty love—Mighty to save!

2
Oh, bliss of the purified! Jesus is mine,
No longer in dread condemnation I pine;
In conscious salvation I sing of his grace,
Who lifted upon me the smiles of his face!—*Cho.*

3
Oh, bliss of the purified! bliss of the pure!
No wound hath the soul that his blood cannot cure;
No sorrow-bowed head but may sweetly find rest,—
No tears but may dry them on Jesus' breast.—*Cho.*

4
O, Jesus, the Crucified! thee will I sing!
My blessed Redeemer! my God and my King!
My soul filled with rapture shall shout o'er the grave,
And triumph at death, in the "Mighty to Save!"—*Cho.*

Copyright, 1867, by *Wm. B. BRADBURY.*
Used from "*Fresh Laurels,*" by per. *Biglow & Main.*

43. I will follow Thee.

Words and Music by JAS. L. ELGINBURG, C. W.

1. I will fol-low thee, my Saviour, Whereso-e'er my lot may be;
Where thou go-est I will fol-low, Yes, my Lord, I'll fol-low thee.

Chorus.
I will fol-low thee, my Saviour; Thou didst shed thy blood for me;
And tho' all men should forsake thee, By thy grace I'll fol-low thee.

2 Tho' the road be rough and thorny,
   Trackless as the foaming sea,
Thou hast trod this way before me,
   And I gladly follow thee.—*Cho.*

3 Tho',tis lone, and dark, and dreary,
   Cheerless though my path may be,
If thy voice I hear before me,
   Fearlessly I'll follow thee.—*Cho.*

4 Though I meet with tribulations,
   Sorely tempted though I be,
I remember thou wast tempted,
   And rejoice to follow thee.—*Cho.*

5 Tho' thou lead'st me thro' affliction,
   Poor, forsaken, though I be,
Thou wast destitute, afflicted,
   And I only follow thee.—*Cho.*

6 Though to Jordan's rolling billows,
   Cold and deep, thou leadest me,
Thou hast cross'd its waves before me,
   And I still will follow thee.—*Cho.*

45. Free.

EDGAR PAGE. — Rev. O. L. CARTER.

1. Many years in bondage, Struggling to be free, Only freed, my Saviour, When I trusted thee.

Chorus. — I am trusting, Lord, in thee: Thy grace is full and free; And as I trust, Thou savest even me.

2
O, what blessed freedom!
  Kept from every snare:
Not a pressing trouble;
  Not a cumb'ring care.
Chorus.—I am trusting, &c.

3
Not a sin to bind me—
  Make me Satan's slave;
But a full salvation
  Which my Jesus gave.
Chorus.—I am trusting, &c.

4
But if thou should'st ask me
  How I came so free:—
Trusting every promise
  Did it all for me.
Chorus.—I am trusting, &c.

46. In the Morning.

Words and Music by Rev. L. HARTSOUGH. *Har. by ALICE HARTSOUGH.*

1. In the morning of the waking, In the dawn of Jubilee year,
When the Master comes for jewels, And in brightness they appear:
I would meet the Saviour smiling, Hear him call me all his own:
I would bear the palm triumphant, Wearing life's eternal crown.

Cho.—In the morning of the waking, In the dawn of Jubilee year,
When the Master comes for Jewels, Then would I with them appear.

2 In the resurrection morning,
And the dead shall all awake;
When the King comes in His beauty,
And in terror earth shall quake;
In the one complete division,
As to right or left we go,
I would hear the Master calling,
"Come, my glory you shall know.

3 In that day of all the others,
That this earth can ever know,
And old Time shall be no longer,
And men go to weal or woe:
May thy right hand be my portion,
That with thee I may abide,
Mingling smiles, and shouts, and praises,
With the blest ones at thy side.

4 Well I know, for thou hast told me,
All this fitness I must gain,
In thy Blood and its lone cleansing,
As my heart yields to thy reign;
Oh! what love did'st thus redeem me,
Oh! what sorrow thou didst bear;
Thus to give me this salvation,
Heav'ns own purity to share.—Cho

Copyright, 1878, by Rev. L. HARTSOUGH.

47. I Will Not Let Thee Go.

Words by "JUNIATA." Music by Rev. W. McDONALD.

1. Let me go; the day is breaking—See, night's shadows hast a-way!
Why should'st thou de-tain me long-er? Loose thy hold, I must a-way!
Let Thee go! No! nev-er, nev-er! Till a bless-ing Thou be-stow;
'Though the sun rise high in heaven, Yet I will not let Thee go!

2
Thy command is, "Be ye holy!"
Now the cleansing blood apply,
From my heart remove the sin-stains;
Jesus, let me feel Thee nigh.
In that precious crimson fountain,
Open'd in Thy wounded side,
Let me plunge, then shall I ever
In Thy perfect love abide.

3
Speak the word, for Thou hast power,
"Be thou clean!" I hear Thee say;
Jesus speaks! 'tis done! oh, glory!
Every stain is wash'd away!
Gladly now I'll do and suffer
All my blessed Master's will:
Come to Jesus; trust him fully;
He his promise will fulfil.

Copyright, 1881, by W. McDONALD.

48. The Stranger at the Door.

Revelations iii, 20.

T. C. O'KANE, by per.

2
O lovely attitude—he stands
With melting heart and loaded hands;
O matchless kindness—and he shows
This matchless kindness to his foes.
Refrain.

3
But will he prove a friend indeed?
He will—the very friend you need.
The friend of sinners? Yes, 'tis he,
With garments dyed on Calvary.
Refrain.

4
Rise, touched with gratitude divine;
Turn out his enemy and thine;
That soul-destroying monster—sin,
And let the Heavenly Stranger in.
Refrain.

5
Admit him, ere his anger burn—
His feet, departed, ne'er return;
Admit him, or the hour's at hand,
You'll at *his* door rejected stand.
Refrain.

50. The Precious Blood.

Words, except 1st verse, by Rev. W. McDonald.
Music and Chorus by Rev. J. H. Stockton.

1. The cross! the cross! the blood-stain'd cross! The hallow'd cross I see!
Re-mind-ing me of precious blood That once was shed for me.

Chorus.
Oh, the blood, the precious blood! That Jesus shed for me,
Up-on the cross, in crimson flood, Just now by faith I see.

2
A thousand, thousand fountains spring
 Up from the throne of God;
But none to me such blessings bring,
 As Jesus' precious blood.—*Cho.*

3
That priceless blood my ransom paid,
 While I in bondage stood;
On Jesus all my sins were laid,
 He sav'd me with his blood.—*Cho.*

4
By faith that blood now sweeps away
 My sins, as like a flood;
Nor lets one guilty blemish stay:
 All praise to Jesus' blood.—*Cho.*

5
This wond'rous theme will best employ
 My harp before my God,
And make all heaven resound with joy,
 For Jesus' cleansing blood.—*Cho.*

51. Wrestling Jacob.

Words by Rev. CHAS. WESLEY.   Arr. by Rev. W. McDONALD.

1. Come, O thou trav-el-ler unknown, Whom still I hold, but can-not see;
My com-pa-ny before is gone, And I am left a-lone with thee;
With thee all night I mean to stay, And wrestle till the break of day, break of day.

2
I need not tell Thee who I am:
My sin and misery declare;
Thyself hast called me by my name;
Look on thy hands, and read it there;
But who, I ask thee, who art thou?
Tell me thy name, and tell me now.

3
In vain thou strugglest to get free;
I never will unloose my hold:
Art thou the Man that died for me?
The secret of thy love unfold:
Wrestling, I will not let thee go,
Till I thy name, thy nature know.

4
Wilt thou not yet to me reveal
Thy new, unutterable name?
Tell me, I still beseech thee, tell;
To know it now resolved I am:
Wrestling, I will not let thee go,
Till I thy name, thy nature know.

5
What tho' my shrinking flesh complain,
And murmur to contend so long?
I rise superior to my pain:
When I am weak, then I am strong;
And when my all of strength shall fail,
I shall with the God-man prevail.

52. VICTORIOUS PRAYER.

1
Yield to me now, for I am weak,
But confident in self-despair;
Speak to my heart, in blessing, speak;
Be conquer'd by my instant prayer;
Speak, or thou never hence shalt move,
And tell me if thy name be Love.

2
'Tis Love! 'tis Love! thou di'dst for me;
I hear thy whisper in my heart;
The morning breaks, the shadows flee;
Pure, universal Love thou art:
To me, to all, thy bowels move,—
Thy nature and thy name is Love.

3
My prayer has pow'r with God; the grace
Unspeakable I now receive;
Through faith I see thee face to face;
I see thee face to face, and live!
In vain I have not wept and strove;
Thy nature and thy name is Love.

4
I know thee, Saviour, who thou art—
Jesus, the feeble sinner's friend;
Nor wilt thou with the night depart,
But stay and love me to the end:
Thy mercies never shall remove;
Thy nature and thy name is Love.

53. Dennis. S. M.

Arr. from H. G. NAGELI.

1. Father, I dare believe Thee merciful and true: Thou wilt my guilty soul forgive,— My fallen soul renew.

2 Come then, for Jesus' sake,
And bid my heart be clean;
An end of all my troubles make,—
An end of all my sin.

3 I cannot wash my heart,
But by believing thee,
And waiting for thy blood t' impart
The spotless purity.

4 While at thy cross I lie,
Jesus, the grace bestow;
Now thy all-cleansing blood apply,
And I am white as snow.

54. GLORIOUS LIBERTY.

1 O, come and dwell in me,
Spirit of power within,
And bring the glorious liberty
From sorrow, fear and sin.

2 The seed of sin's disease,
Spirit of health, remove—
Spirit of finish'd holiness,
Spirit of perfect love.

3 Hasten the joyful day
Which shall my sins consume;
When old things shall be done away
And all things new become.

4 I want the witness, Lord,
That all I do is right—
According to thy will and word—
Well pleasing in thy sight.

5 I ask no higher state,
Indulge me but in this,
And soon or later then translate
To my eternal bliss.

55. FOR DILIGENCE AND WATCHFULNESS.

1 A charge to keep I have,
A God to glorify,
A never-dying soul to save,
And fit it for the sky.

2 To serve the present age,
My calling to fulfil,
O, may it all my powers engage
To do my Master's will.

3 Arm me with jealous care,
As in thy sight to live,
And oh, thy servant, Lord, prepare
A strict account to give.

4 Help me to watch and pray,
And on thyself rely,
Assured if I my trust betray
I shall forever die.

56. EMBRACING THE ALL-SUFFICIENT PORTION.

1 And can I yet delay
My little all to give?
To tear my soul from earth away
For Jesus to receive?

2 Nay, but I yield, I yield!
I can hold out no more:
I sink, by dying love compell'd,
And own thee conqueror!

3 Though late, I all forsake,
My friends, my all resign;
Gracious Redeemer, take, oh! take
And seal me ever thine.

4 Come, and possess me whole,
Nor hence again remove;
Settle and fix my wav'ring soul
With all thy weight of love.

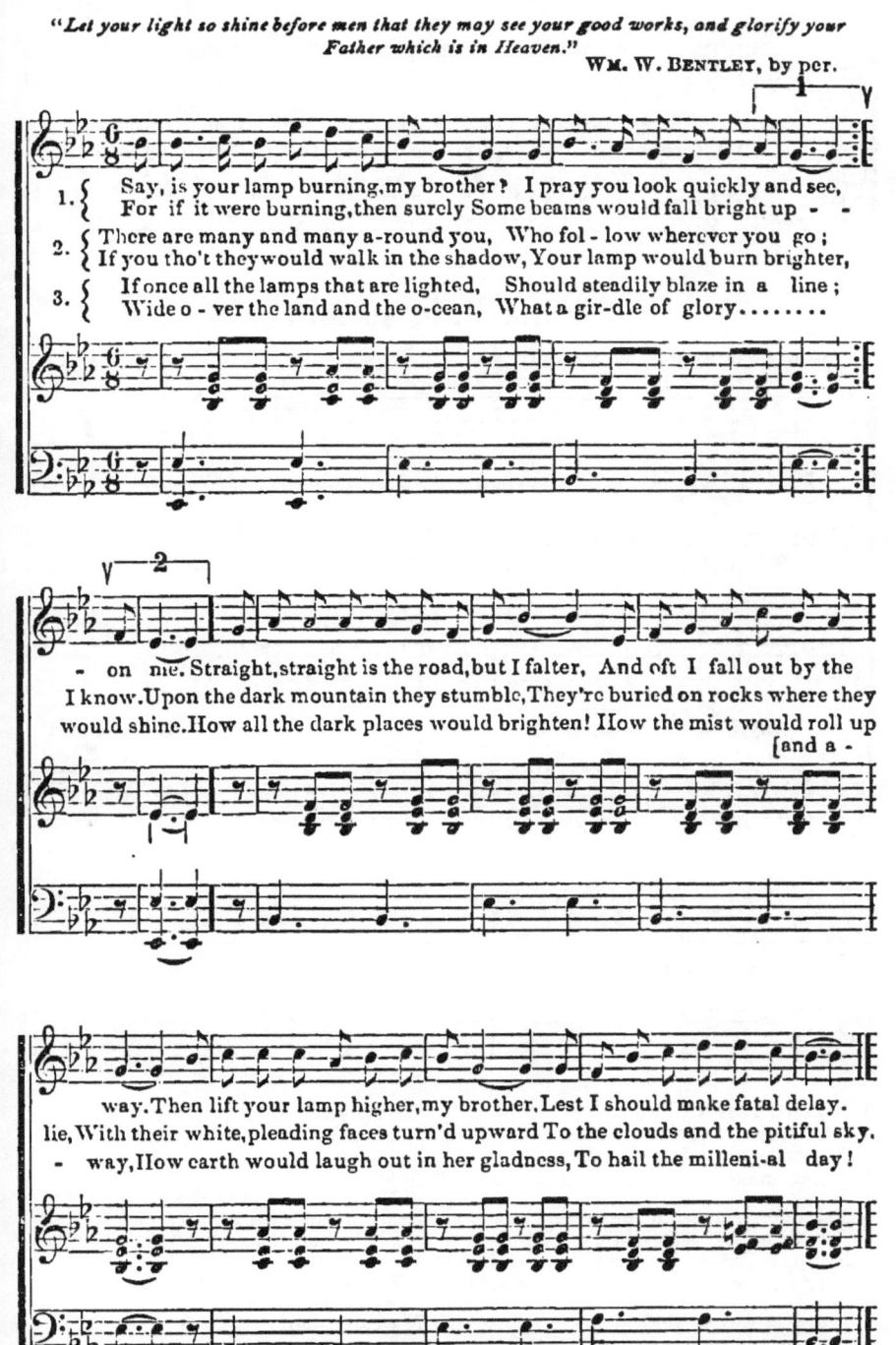

Is your Lamp Burning? Concluded.

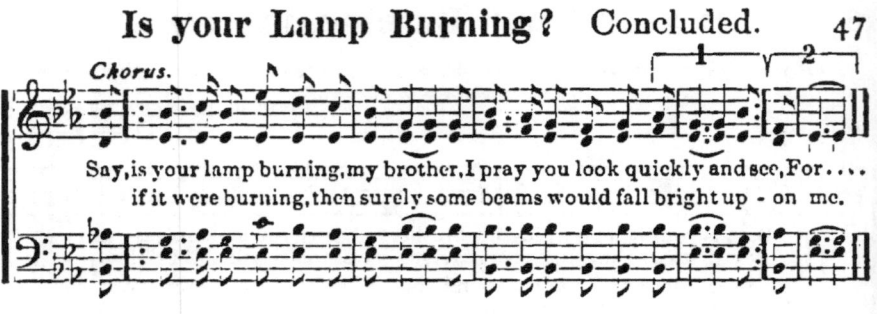

Say, is your lamp burning, my brother, I pray you look quickly and see, For
if it were burning, then surely some beams would fall bright up-on me.

58. Jesus Paid it All.

Words arr. by Rev. W. McDonald.   J. T. Grape.

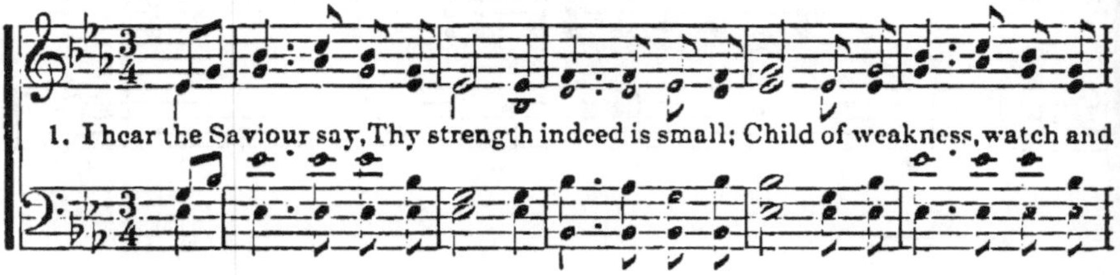

1. I hear the Saviour say, Thy strength indeed is small; Child of weakness, watch and pray, Find in me thine all in all.

Chorus.
Je-sus paid it all: All to him I owe; Sin had left a crimson stain; He wash'd it white as snow.

2 O Lord, at last I find
   Thy pow'r, and thine alone,
Can change this heart of mine,
   And make it all thine own.—*Cho.*

3 Then down beneath the cross,
   I lay my sin-sick soul;
Nothing I bring but dross,
   Thy grace must make me whole.—*Cho.*

4 I now in Christ abide—
   In him is perfect rest;
Close sheltered in his side,
   I am divinely blest.—*Cho.*

5 When at my post I fall,
   My ransom'd soul shall rise;
And "Jesus paid it all,"
   Shall rend the vaulted skies.—*Cho.*

6 And when, in heav'n above,
   At Jesus' feet I fall,
My song shall ever be—
   Jesus has paid it all.—*Cho.*

62 Lights along the Shore.

Words by Rev. J. H. STOCKTON. (By Permission.) Arr. by W. G. FISCHER.

1. I'm a pilgrim and a stranger passing over,
The road may be rough, but 'tis clear,
And a starry crown awaits me o'er the river,
And Jesus bids me welcome there.

Chorus.

There are lights along the shore that never grow dim,
That never, never grow dim;
These souls are all aflame with the love of Jesus' name,
They guide us, yes, they guide us unto him.

2 Sometimes I meet with trials on my journey,
   Temptation and sorrow by the way:
   But Jesus speaks, and says "I'm ever near thee,
   To guide to realms of endless day."—*Chorus.*

3 Friends of Jesus! may your lights be trimm'd and burning,
   And shining along the way of love;
   Soon you'll gain the heights of glory, and be singing
   The happy song of saints above.—*Chorus.*

4 We're a happy band of Christians, bound for Canaan,
   The land is in view, the wind's fair;
   We will sing redeeming love beyond the Jordan,
   With Jesus dwell forever there.—*Chorus.*

63. More like Thee.

51

Words and Music by W. J. KIRKPATRICK, by per.

1. Jesus, Saviour, great Example,
Pattern of all purity,
I would follow in thy footsteps,
Daily growing more like thee.

Chorus.
More like thee, more like thee,
Saviour, this my constant pray'r shall be,—
Day by day, where'er I stay,
Make me more and more like thee.

2
Lest I wander from thy pathway,
Or my feet move wearily,
Saviour, take my hand and lead me,
Keep me steadfast: more like thee.

3
When temptations fiercely lower,
And my shrinking soul would flee,
Change each weakness into power,
Keep me spotless: more like thee.

4
When around me all is darkness,
And thy beauties none may see,
May thy beams, O Glorious Brightness,
In effulgence shine through me.

5
When death's cold, repulsive finger
Leaves its impress on my brow,
May thy life, within me swelling,
Keep me singing then as now.

Copyright, 1876, by W. J. KIRKPATRICK.

65. And Can It Be?

Arranged by WM. G. FISCHER.

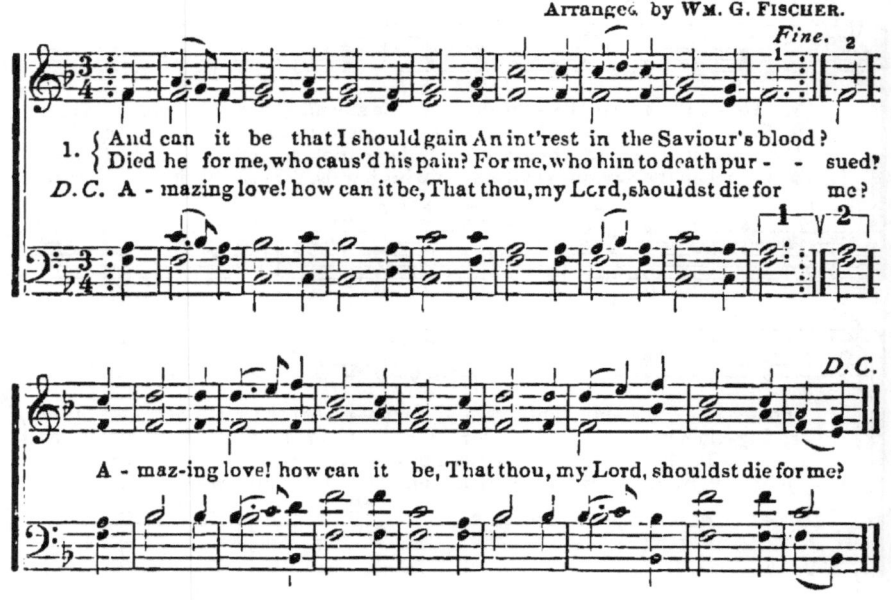

1. And can it be that I should gain An int'rest in the Saviour's blood?
Died he for me, who caus'd his pain? For me, who him to death pur-sued?
D.C. A-mazing love! how can it be, That thou, my Lord, shouldst die for me?

2
'Tis myst'ry all, th' Immortal dies!
 Who can explore his strange design?
In vain the first-born seraph tries
 To sound the depths of love divine;
'Tis mercy all! let earth adore:
Let angel minds inquire no more.

3
He left his Father's throne above:
 (So free, so infinite his grace!)
Emptied himself of all but love,
 And bled for Adam's helpless race ;
'Tis mercy all, immense and free,
For O, my God, it found out me!

4
Long my imprison'd spirit lay,
 Fast bound in sin and nature's night;
Thine eye diffused a quick'ning ray ;
 I woke: the dungeon flam'd with light;
My chains fell off, my heart was free—
I rose, went forth, and follow'd thee.

5
No condemnation now I dread,
 Jesus, with all in him is mine;
Alive in him my living Head,
 And cloth'd in right'ousness divine,
Bold I approach th' eternal throne,
And claim the crown thro' Christ my own.

66. BELIEVING AGAINST HOPE.

1 Away, my unbelieving fear!
 Fear shall in me no more have place;
My Saviour doth not yet appear—
 He hides the brightness of his face ;
But shall I therefore let him go,
 And basely to the tempter yield ?
No, in the strength of Jesus, no.
 I never will give up my shield.

2 Although the vine its fruit deny,
 Although the olive yield no oil,
The with'ring fig trees droop and die,
 The fields elude the tiller's toil,
The empty stall no herd afford,
 And perish all the bleating race,
Yet will I triumph in the Lord,
 The God of my salvation praise.

3 In hope, believing against hope,
 Jesus, my Lord, my God, I claim ;
Jesus, my strength, shall lift me up ;
 Salvation is in Jesus' name.
To me he soon shall bring it nigh ;
 My soul shall then outstrip the wind;
On wings of love mount up on high,
 And leave the world and sin behind.

67 Skeptic, spare that Book.

Arr. by Rev. W. McDonald.

1. O skeptic, spare that book! Touch not a single leaf; Nor on its pages look With eyes of unbelief. 'Twas my forefathers' stay, In hours of agony; O skeptic, go thy way, And let that old book be.

2 That good old book of life,
  For centuries hath stood;
Unharm'd amidst the strife,
  When earth was drunk with blood.
And wouldst thou harm it now,
  Or have its truths forgot?
O skeptic, go thy way,
  Thy hand shall harm it not.

3 Its very name recalls
  The happy hours of youth,
When in my grandsire's halls,
  I heard its tales of truth.

I've seen his white hair flow
  O'er the volume as he read,
But that was long ago,
  And the good old man is dead.

4 My dear grandmother, too,
  When I was but a boy,
I've seen her eyes of blue
  Weep o'er it tears of joy.
Her tears they linger still,
  And dear they are to me:
O skeptic, go thy way,
  And let that old book be.

Copyright, 1873, by Rev. W. McDonald.

68. Home beyond the Tide.

Arr. for this Work. Rev. C. H. DUNBAR.

1. We are out on the o-cean sailing, Homeward bound we sweetly glide,
We are out on the o-cean sail-ing, To our home be-yond the tide.

Chorus.
All the storms will soon be o-ver, Then we'll an-chor in the harbor,
We are out on the o-cean sail-ing, To our home be-yond the tide.

2
Millions now are safely landed
Over on the golden shore;
Millions more are on the journey,
Yet there's room for millions more.
Cho.—All the storms, &c.

3
Come on board, oh ship for glory,
Be in haste, make up your mind,
For your vessel's weighing anchor,
You will soon be left behind.
Cho.—All the storms, &c.

4
When we all are safely anchor'd,
We will shout our journey o'er;
We will walk about the city,
And will sing forevermore.
Cho.—All the storms, &c.

69 My Heart-Song.

By per. of PHILIP PHILLIPS. Words and Music by Rev. L. HARTSOUGH.

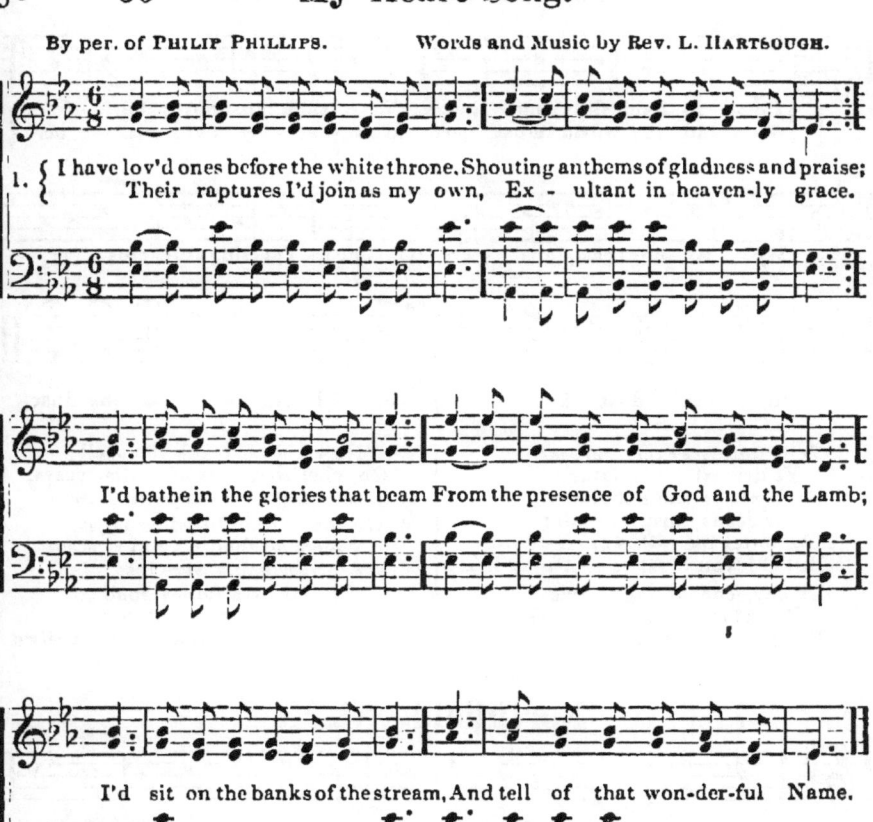

1. I have lov'd ones before the white throne, Shouting anthems of gladness and praise;
Their raptures I'd join as my own, Exultant in heaven-ly grace.
I'd bathe in the glories that beam From the presence of God and the Lamb;
I'd sit on the banks of the stream, And tell of that wonderful Name.

2
I'd tell of the power of sin,
　How fallen my soul had become;
How hopeless and cheerless within,
　While recklessly wand'ring from home.
Thus burden'd with sin and its woe,
　My vileness was all I could see,
When Jesus said, go with me, go,
　Thy soul from its sorrows I'll free.

3
I gave him my poor fainting heart,
　And quickly salvation received;
I felt his dear life in each part,
　As I in his mercy believed.
Blessed Saviour, now seal me thine own,
　Thine image stamp wholly in me;
My heart, be it ever thy throne,
　From sin keep it evermore free.

4
Henceforth this vain world must all go,
　Its claims I can see are but dross,
For none but my Jesus I'll know,
　I'll glory alone in the cross.
I am thine, blessed Jesus, all thine,
　The witness impart unto me;
The death that I die is to sin,
　The life that I live is to thee.

5
Go, friends that would keep me from Him!
　Go, joys that would share with his love!
Go, hopes that would draw me to sin,
　Go, all, that from him would remove!
Come, sorrow, if only in thee
　I shall cling to my Saviour and God;
Come, scorn and reproach, if left free
　To be drawn evermore to my Lord.

70. Christ received by Faith.

1. Come, my fond flutt'ring heart, Come, thou must now be free:
Thou and the world must part, How-ev-er hard it be.

My weeping pas-sions own 'tis just, Yet cling still clos-er

to the dust, Yet cling.... still clos-er to the dust.

2 Ye tempting sweets, forbear,
Ye dearest idols, fall,
My heart ye can not share,
For Jesus must have all;
'Tis bitter pain—'tis cruel smart,
But O! you must consent, my heart.

3 Ye gay, enchanting throng,
Ye golden dreams, farewell!
Earth hath prevail'd too long,
Now I must break the spell;
Go, cherish'd joys of earlier years,
Jesus, forgive these parting tears.

4 Welcome, thou bleeding cross,
Welcome, thou way to God;
My former gains were loss,
My path was follies' road;
At last my heart is undeceiv'd,
The world is giv'n, and God receiv'd.

71. Northfield. C. M.

1 I know that my Redeemer lives,
And ever prays for me;
A token of his love he gives—
A pledge of liberty.

2 I find him lifting up my head:
He brings salvation near;
His presence makes me free indeed,
And he will soon appear.

3 He wills that I should holy be!
What can withstand his will?
The counsel of his grace in me
He surely shall fulfil.

4 Jesus, I hang upon thy word;
I steadfastly believe
Thou wilt return and claim me, Lord,
And to thyself receive.

5 When God is mine, and I am his,
Of paradise possess'd,
I tast unutterable bliss
And everlasting rest.

72

1 Jesus, united by thy grace,
And each to each endear'd,
With confidence we seek thy face,
And know our prayer is heard.

2 Still let us own our common Lord,
And bear thine easy yoke—
A band of love, a threefold chord,
Which never can be broke.

3 Make us into one spirit drink;
Baptize into thy name;
And let us always kindly think
And sweetly speak the same.

4 Touch'd by the loadstone of thy love,
Let all our hearts agree;
And ever toward each other move,
And ever move toward thee.

5 To thee, inseparably join'd,
Let all our spirits cleave;
O may we all the loving mind
That was in thee receive.

73 The Valley of Blessing.

Mrs. ANNIE WITTENMEYER.   WM. G. FISCHER, by per.

1. I have entered the val-ley of blessing so sweet, And Je-sus a-bides with me there; And his spir-it and blood make my cleansing complete, And his per-fect love casteth out fear.

Chorus.

Oh come to this val-ley of blessing so sweet, Where Je-sus will fullness be-stow— And be-lieve, and receive, and confess him, That all his sal-va-tion may know.

2 There is peace in the valley of blessing so sweet,
   And plenty the land doth impart,
And there's rest for the weary worn traveler's feet,
   And joy for the sorrowing heart.—*Chorus.*

3 There is love in the valley of blessing so sweet,
   Such as none but the blood-wash'd may feel,
When heaven comes down redeemed spirits to greet,
   And Christ sets his covenant seal.—*Chorus.*

4 There's a song in the valley of blessing so sweet,
   That angels would fain join the strain,
As with rapturous praises we bow at his feet,
   Crying "Worthy the Lamb that was slain!"—*Chorus.*

74   Coronation.   C. M.
OLIVER HOLDEN.

1 All hail the pow'r of Jesus' name!
   Let angels prostrate fall;
  Bring forth the royal diadem,
   And crown him Lord of all.

2 Ye chosen seed of Israel's race,
   Ye ransom'd from the fall,
  Hail him who saves you by his grace,
   And crown him Lord of all.

3 Sinners, whose love can ne'er forget
   The wormwood and the gall;
  Go, spread your trophies at his feet,
   And crown him Lord of all.

4 Let every kindred, every tribe,
   On this terrestrial ball,
  To him all majesty ascribe,
   And crown him Lord of all.

5 O that with yonder sacred throng
   We at his feet may fall;
  We'll join the everlasting song,
   And crown him Lord of all.

---

75   Azmon.   C. M.
From GLAZER.

1 Jesus hath died that I might live,
   Might live to God alone;
  In him eternal life receive,
   And be in spirit one.

2 Saviour, I thank thee for the grace,
   The gift unspeakable,
  And wait with arms of faith t' embrace,
   And all thy love to feel.

3 My soul breaks out in strong desire,
   The perfect bliss to prove;
  My longing heart is all on fire,
   To be dissolved in love.

4 Give me thyself; from every boast,
   From every wish set free;
  Let all I am in thee be lost,
   But give thyself to me.

5 Thy gifts, alas! cannot suffice,
   Unless thyself be giv'n;
  Thy presence makes my paradise,
   And where thou art is heaven.

---

76   Balerma.   C. M.

1 Come, let us use the grace divine,
   And all, with one accord,
  In a perpetual cov'nant join
   Ourselves to Christ the Lord:—

2 Give up ourselves thro' Jesus' pow'r,
   His name to glorify,
  And promise, in this sacred hour,
   For God to live and die.

3 The cov'nant we this moment mak ,
   Be ever kept in mind;
  We will no more our God forsake,
   Or cast his words behind.

4 We never will throw off his fear,
   Who hears our solemn vow;
  And if thou art well pleased to hear
   Come down and meet us now.

5 Thee, Father, Son, and Holy Ghost,
   Let all our hearts receive;
  Present with the celestial host,
   The peaceful answer give.

6 To each the cov'nant blood apply,
   Which takes our sins away,
  And register our names on high,
   And keep us to that day.

77. Royal Way of the Cross.

Rev. L. HARTSOUGH.

1. We may spread our couch with ro-ses, And sleep thro' the summer day;
But the soul that in sloth re-pos-es, Is not in the nar-row way.
D.C. For the roy-al way to heav-en Is the roy-al way of the cross.

If we fol-low the chart that is giv-en, We need not be at a loss,

2 To one who is rear'd in splendor,
　The cross is a heavy load,
And the feet that are soft and tender
　Will shrink from the thorny road;
But the chains of the soul must be riven,
　And wealth must be as dross,
For the royal way to heaven
　Is the royal way of the cross.

3 We say we will walk to-morrow
　The path we refuse to-day,
And still with our lukewarm sorrow
　We shrink from the narrow way.
What heeded the chosen eleven
　How the fortunes of life might toss.
As they follow'd their Master to heaven
　By the royal way of the cross?

78. Rock of Ages.

Dr. HASTINGS.

1 Rock of Ages, cleft for me,
　Let me hide myself in thee;
　Let the water and the blood,
　From thy wounded side which flow'd,
　Be of sin a double cure,
　Save from wrath and make me pure.
2 Could my tears forever flow,
　Could my zeal no languor know;
　These for sin could not atone;
　Thou must save, and thou alone:
　In my hand no price I bring,
　Simply to thy cross I cling.
3 While I draw this fleeting breath,
　When my eyes shall close in death,
　When I rise to worlds unknown,
　And behold thee on thy throne,
　Rock of Ages, cleft for me,
　Let me hide myself in thee.

79. ENTIRE CONSECRATION.

1 Father, Son, and Holy Ghost,
　One in three, and three in one,
As by the celestial host,
　Let thy will on earth be done;
Praise by all to thee be given,
Gracious Lord of earth and heaven!
2 If so poor a worm as I,
　May to thy great glory live,
All my actions sanctify,
　All my words and thoughts receive;
Claim me for thy service, claim
All I have, and all I am.

3 Take my soul and body's powers:
　Take my mem'ry, mind, and will:
All my goods, and all my hours,
　All I know, and all I feel;
All I think, or speak, or do;
Take my heart, but make it new!
4 Now, my God, thine own I am,
　Now I give thee back thine own:
Freedom, friends, and health and fame,
　Consecrate to thee alone:
Thine I live, thrice happy I!
Happier still if thine I die.

Streaming Mercy.

Arr. for this Work.

1. Drooping souls, no longer grieve, Heaven is propitious.
If on Christ you do believe, You will find him precious
Jesus now is passing by, Calling mourners to him;
He has died for you and I, Now look up and view him.

2
From his hands, his feet, his side,
　Flows a healing fountain;
See the consolation tide,
　Boundless as the ocean.
See the living waters move,
　For the sick and dying;
Now resolve to gain his love,
　Or to perish trying.

3
Streaming mercy how it flows,
　Now I know I feel it;
Half has never yet been told,
　Yet I want to tell it.
Jesus' blood has healed my wounds,
　Oh the wondrous story!
I was lost, but now am found,
　Glory! glory! glory!

81. We'll bear the Cross.

Words by FANNIE CROSBY.   Music by W. G. FISCHER, by per.

1. No love to give, no tears to weep, No cross for him to bear, Whose an-guish lav'd in drops of blood That lone-ly midnight prayer.

Chorus. Oh, wel-come sor-row, toil, reproach, What-e'er our cross may be; With joy, thou precious Lamb of God, We'll bear the cross for thee.

2
Shall Jesus wear the cruel thorns,
  And yet no pain be ours;
Must he a path of suff'ring tread,
  And we a path of flow'rs?
    Chorus.—O welcome sorrow, &c.

3
Dear Saviour, in thy glorious name,
  Our every foe we'll face,
We'll fight like soldiers in thy cause,
  And conquer by thy grace.
    Chorus.—O welcome sorrow, &c.

4
Yet, till our latest moment come,
  Thy cross on earth we'll bear;
Then rise victorious through thy blood,
  A heavenly crown to wear.
    Chorus.—O welcome sorrow, &c.

Heart Longings.

"I do not want one thought that is not fit for Heaven."—If I see one passing the street who causes a wrong thought, I think how would that look in heaven."—See Bishop Hamlin's Life, p. 516.

Words and Music by Rev. L. HARTSOUGH. Har. by Miss ALICE HARTSOUGH.

1. "I do not want one tho't," dear Lord, "That is not fit for Heav'n,"
May ev-'ry wish and hope I have, By Thee, to me be giv'n;
I want no vis-ion but the pure On High would all ad-mire;
What an-gel minds would blush to know, That I would not de-sire.

2 No words I'd speak, would cause Thee pain,
   Or e'en the least regret;
No deeds attempt Thou wouldst not do:
   Lord, keep me at Thy feet.
A tender eye, a shrinking heart,
   All owned and filled by Thee,
Would meet the highest wish I have:
   O make me, keep me free.

3 No step I'd take, but only there
   Where God's dear Spirit leads;
No route to press my feet along,
   But where are holy deeds.
Thy hand, Thy hand, dear Saviour, now,
   Must evermore clasp mine;
So I move on in all Thy ways,
   Forever, wholly, Thine.

4 But how can such a worm as I,
   So purely walk, and free?
Or, how can such a heart as mine,
   Turn wholly, Lord, to Thee?
Thou, Thou alone canst make the change
   And fill the Throne within;
Control the springs of thought and deed,
   And cleanse, and keep me clean.

Copyright, 1877, by Rev. L. HARTSOUGH.

83 I've been Redeemed.

As sung by the Tennesseeans.

Arr. by Dr. T. J. PEACOCK.

1. There is a fountain fill'd with blood, Drawn from Immanuel's veins,
And sinners plung'd beneath that flood, Lose all their guilty stains.

Chorus.

I've been re-deem'd........ I've been re-deem'd........ I've been re-deem'd.... I've been re-deem'd...... I've been re-deem'd....... I've been re-deem'd......... Been wash'd in the blood of the Lamb. Been re-

I've been re-deem'd, I've been re-deem'd, I've been redeem'd, I've been redeem'd, I've been redeem'd, I've been redeem'd,

Fine.

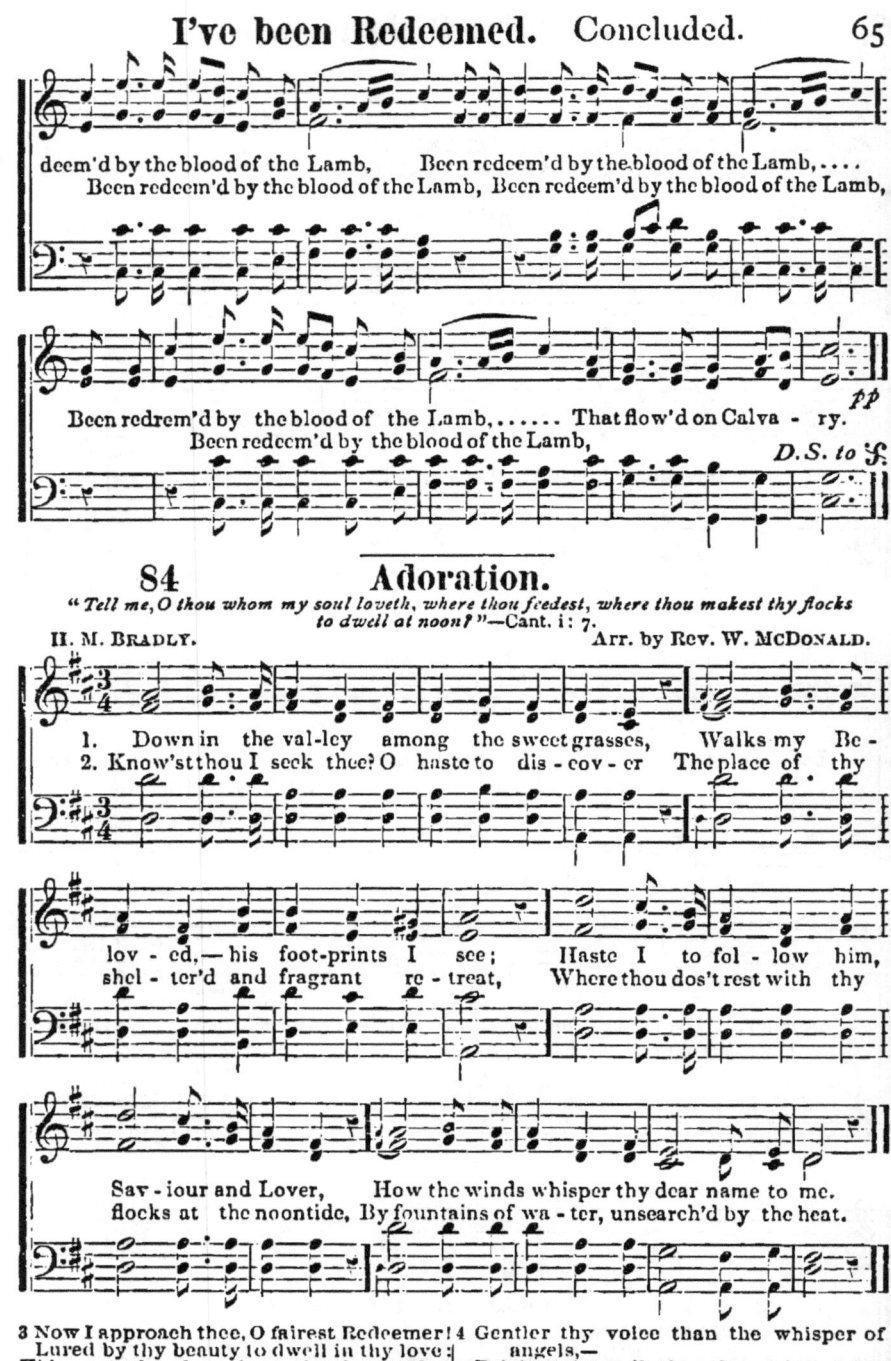

85. Waiting at the Pool.

Rev. A. J. HOUGH. WM. G. FISCHER, by per.

1. Thousands stand to-day in sorrow, Waiting at the pool; Say-ing they will wash to-mor-row, Waiting at the pool; Oth-ers step in left and right, Wash their stained garments white, Leaving you in sorrow's night, Waiting at the pool, Wait-ing, Wait-ing, Waiting at the pool.

2 Souls, your filthy garments wearing,
　Waiting at the pool ;
Hearts, your heavy burden bearing,
　Waiting at the pool ;
Can it be you never heard,
Jesus long ago hath stirred
The waters with his mighty word,
　Waiting at the pool?

3 Thousands once were standing near you,
　Waiting at the pool ;
Come their voices back to cheer you,
　Waiting at the pool :
Back from Canaan's happy shore,
Sorrows past and labor o'er,
Where they stand in tears no more,
　Waiting at the pool.

4 Mother leaves the son, the daughter,
　Waiting at the pool ;
Calls to them across the water,
　Waiting at the pool ;
You can never more embrace
Mother, or behold her face,
If you keep the leper's place,
　Waiting at the pool.

5 Step in boldly—death may smite you,
　Waiting at the pool ;
Jesus may no more invite you,
　Waiting at the pool ;
Faith is near you, take her hand,
Seek with her the better land,
And no longer doubting stand
　Waiting at the pool.

Copyright, 1877, by Wm. G. FISCHER.

3
We're going home with saints to be,
Where dwell our friends we long to see,
To join the glorious ransomed band
Which stands in bliss at God's right hand.
4
How sweet, amid life's toils and fears,
To know that Jesus always hears;
In darkest night he bids us come,
And all our fears and wants make known.

5
We'll cling to Jesus in the hour
When Sin and Satan use their pow'r,
And murmur not when sorrows come,
For by-and-by we're going home.
6
No dying groans shall then be heard,
And we shall speak no parting word;
O! sinner, to our Saviour come,
And join the band that's going home.

88. The Child of a King.

HATTIE E. BUEL.
By per. Barrett Bros.
REV. JOHN B. SUMNER.
Arr. for this Work.

1. My Father is rich in houses and lands, He holdeth the wealth of the world in his hands! Of ru-bies and diamonds, of sil-ver and gold, His cof-fers are full; He has rich-es un-told! I'm the child of a King, the child of a King! With Jesus, my Saviour, I'm the child of a King!

2 My Father's own Son, the Saviour of men!
Once wandered on earth, the poorest of them;
But now He is reigning in glory on High,
And will give me a home with himself by-and-by.—*Cho.*

3 I once was an outcast, a stranger on earth,
A sinner from choice, and an *alien* by birth;
But I've been *adopted*, my name's written down;
An heir to a mansion, a robe and a crown.—*Cho.*

4 A tent or a cottage, why should I care?
They're building a palace for me over there!
Though exiled from home, yet, still I can sing,
All glory to God, I'm the child of a King.—*Cho.*

89. Cleanse me, O Lord.

From "Gospel Singer,"
By per. of PHILIP PHILLIPS.   Words and Music by Rev. L. HARTSOUGH.

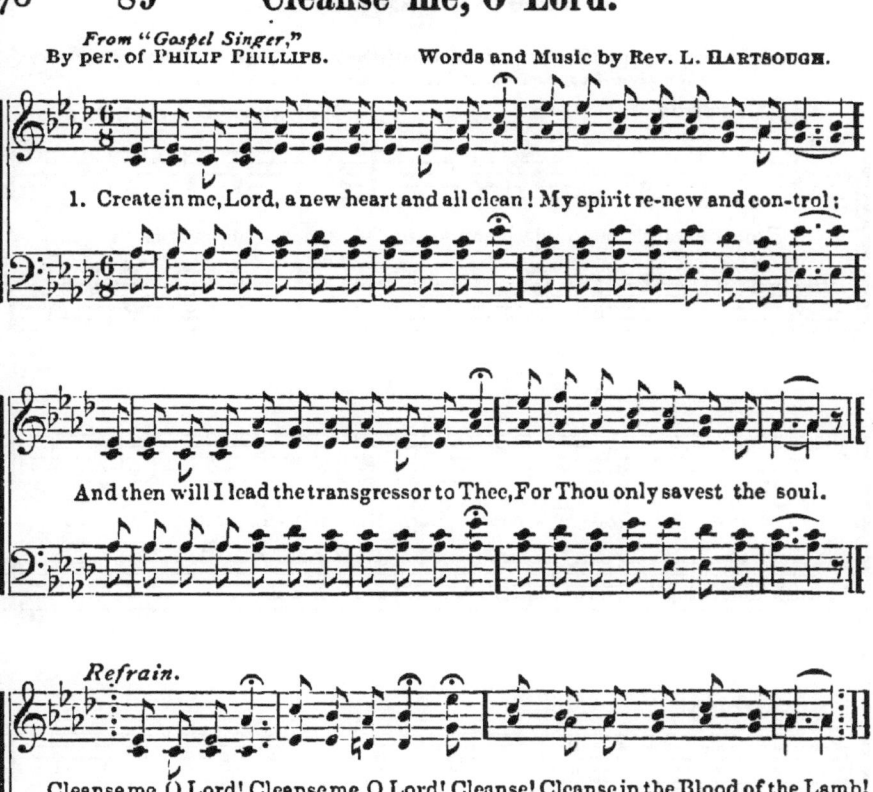

1. Create in me, Lord, a new heart and all clean! My spirit re-new and con-trol;
And then will I lead the transgressor to Thee, For Thou only savest the soul.

Refrain.
Cleanse me, O Lord! Cleanse me, O Lord! Cleanse! Cleanse in the Blood of the Lamb!

2
My sins though as scarlet, make white in the Blood,
  Thou'st promised to cleanse them as snow;
Though red, like to crimson, oh! make them as wool,
  Thy Love is sufficient I know.—*Refrain.*

3
In David's glad House is the Fountain prepared,
  It flows for uncleanness and sin;
Oh! help me, dear Lord, its great virtues to test,
  Oh! wash me without, and within.—*Refrain.*

4
To Thee I am coming, confessing my want,
  Thy faithfulness, Lord, I believe;
My guilt put away, and then cleanse me, dear Lord,
  Thine uttermost grace I'd receive.—*Refrain.*

5
The Gift of thy Power—a baptismal fire—
  My Pentecost let it now be;
Thus sealed as I'm cleansed, and henceforth to be Thine,
  Forever kept only by Thee.—*Refrain.*

90. Whosoever Believeth.

"For God so loved the world, that he gave his only begotten Son, that whosoever believeth in him should not perish, but have everlasting life."—John 3: 16.

Rev. F. DENISON.   W. WARREN BENTLEY, by per.

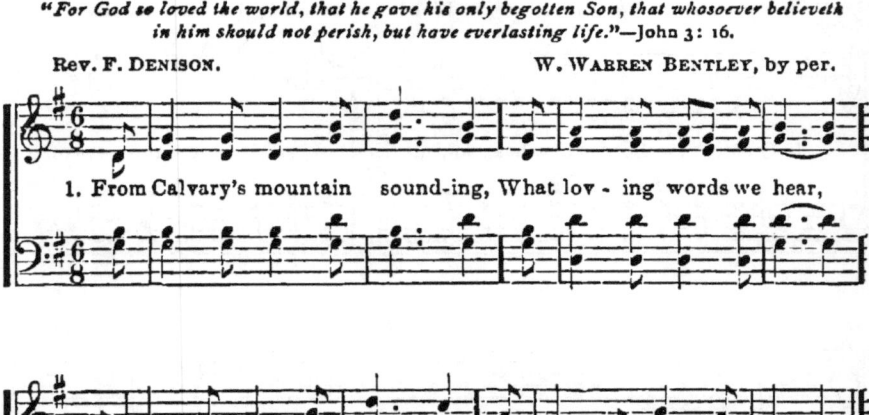

1. From Calvary's mountain sound-ing, What lov-ing words we hear,

The love of God a-bound-ing, Dis-pell-ing all our fear.

Refrain.

Who-so-ev-er be-liev-eth, Who-so-ev-er be-liev-eth,

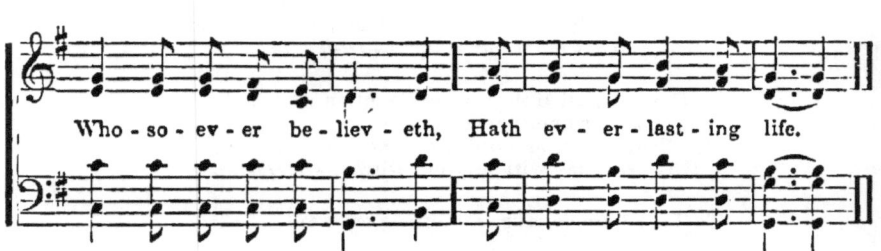

Who-so-ev-er be-liev-eth, Hath ev-er-last-ing life.

2
Whoe'er my word believeth,
  We hear the Saviour say,
A pardon full receiveth,
  All sins are wash'd away.
Refrain.—Whosoever believeth, &c.

3
O, brother, come and trust him,
  O, come to him to-day;
He's waiting to receive you,
  Why longer then delay.
Refrain.—Whosoever believeth, &c.

91. The Open Gate.

Words by an English Sailor.
S. J. VAIL. From "*Singing Annual*,"
By per. of PHILIP PHILLIPS.

1. There is a gate stands so-pen wide, And, thro' its portals gleaming,
A radiance from the Cross a-far The Saviour's love re-veal-ing.

Refrain.
Oh! depths of mer-cy! can it be That gate stands o-pen wide for me?
Stands o-pen wide both night and day, Stands o-pen wide for me?

2
It open stands for old and young,
Though filled with joy or sorrow;
The Spirit wooes your souls along,
The gate may close to-morrow.
Refrain.—Oh, depths of mercy! &c.

3
O, sinner, waken from your guilt,
Nor let your heart deceive you;
For you the blood of Christ was spilt,
He's waiting to receive you.
Refrain.—Oh, depths of mercy! &c.

4
O, blessed Spirit, lead me in,
And let me falter never;
Make me a victor over sin,—
I'll praise thee then forever.
Refrain.—Oh, depths of mercy! &c.

92. Our Loved Ones in Heaven.

Words by Rev. J. W. DADMUN. Music by LESSUR.

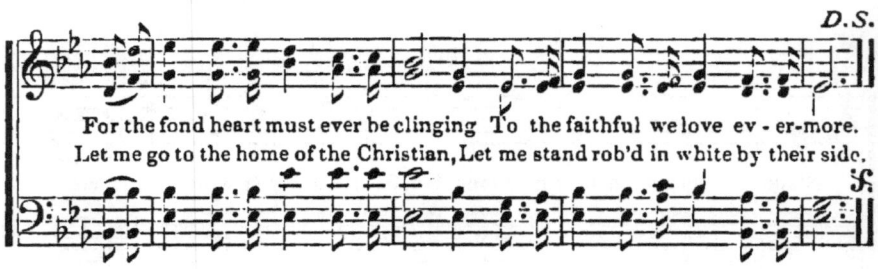

2
There endless springs of life are flowing,
  There are the fields of living green;
Mansions of beauty are provided,
  And the King of the saints is seen.
Soon my conflicts and toils will be ended;
  I shall join those who've pass'd on before;
For my loved ones, O how I do miss them!
  I must press on and meet them once more.
    Chorus.—O, the prospect, &c.

3
Faith now beholds the flowing river,
  Coming from underneath the throne;
There, too, the Saviour reigns forever,
  And he'll welcome the faithful home.
Would you sit by the banks of the river
  With the friends you have lov'd by your side?
Would you join in the song of the angels?
  Then be ready to follow your guide
    Chorus.—O, the prospect, &c.

93 Hallelujah, Jesus Saves.

"Him that cometh to me I will in no wise cast out."—John 6: 37.

Rev. A. J. HOUGH. Mrs. J. F. KNAPP, by per.

1. Many at the cross are kneeling, Jesus, Jesus saves,
By his boundless love revealing, Jesus, Jesus saves.

Chorus.
Hallelujah, light is beaming, Hallelujah, blood is streaming,
Hallelujah, Jesus saves, Hallelujah, Jesus saves.

2
All the lost and all the lonely,
  Jesus, Jesus saves,
Oh, come now, believing only
  Jesus, Jesus saves.—*Cho.*

3
Hearts are at this moment proving,
  Jesus, Jesus saves,
Every sinful stain removing,
  Jesus, Jesus saves.—*Cho.*

4
Come with tears your sin confessing,
  Jesus, Jesus saves,
Seek and find the choicest blessing,
  Jesus, Jesus saves.—*Cho.*

5
Hallelujah, saints are singing,
  Jesus, Jesus saves,
Heav'n, with joyous song is ringing,
  Jesus, Jesus saves.—*Cho.*

A Home Over There.

2
O think of the friends over there,
  Who before us the journey have trod;
Of the songs that they breathe on the air,
  In their home in the palace of God.
Over there, over there,
O think of the friends over there.—*Cho.*

3
I'll soon be at home over there,
  For the end of my journey I see;
Many dear to my heart over there
  Are watching and waiting for me.
Over there, over there,
I'll soon be at home over there.—*Cho.*

95. Only in the Name of Jesus.

"If ye shall ask anything in my name, I will do it."—Jno. 14: 14.

J. E. RANKIN, D. D. E. S. LORENZ, by per.

1. There is peace only in His name, Only in the name of Jesus;
And that peace, wretched souls may claim, Only in the name of Jesus!

2. There is strength only in His name, Only in the name of Jesus;
And man can his wild passions tame, Only in the name of Jesus,

Chorus.
Name of Jesus, Name of Jesus! When you pray, O pray in His name, Go to God with ev-'ry care; Tell it to Him in your pray'r, Only in the name of Jesus.

3 Tell to God, what your sins have been,
Only in the name of Jesus;
He can make you all pure within,
Only in the name of Jesus.
Chorus.—Name of Jesus, &c.

4 Tell to God what your weakness is,
Only in the name of Jesus.
He is strong, and to help is His,
Only in the name of Jesus.
Chorus.—Name of Jesus, &c.

96. Glory to His Name.

"I will glorify Thy Name forevermore." —Ps. 63: 4.

Rev. ELISHA HOFFMAN. Rev. J. H. STOCKTON.

1. Down at the cross where my Saviour died, Down, where for cleansing from sin I cried; There to my heart was the blood applied; Glory to His name.

Chorus.
Glo-ry to His name. Glo-ry to His name. There to my heart was the blood ap-plied. Glo-ry to His name.

2
I am so wondrously sav'd from sin,
Jesus so sweetly abides within:
There at the cross where He took me in.
  Glory to His name.
Chorus.—Glory to His name, &c.

3
Oh, precious fountain, that saves from sin,
I am so glad I have enter'd in ;
There Jesus saves me and keeps me clean,
  Glory to His name.
Chorus.—Glory to His name, &c.

4
Come to this fountain, so rich and sweet;
Cast thy poor soul at the Saviour's feet;
Plunge in to-day, and be made complete;
  Glory to His name.
Chorus.—Glory to His name, &c.

97 The Sinner Invited.

Words arr. by Rev. W. McDonald.　　Arr. by Rev. W. McDonald.

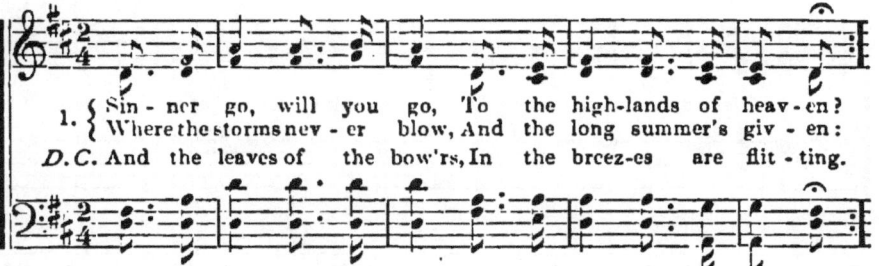

1. Sin-ner go, will you go, To the high-lands of heav-en?
  Where the storms nev-er blow, And the long summer's giv-en:
D.C. And the leaves of the bow'rs, In the breez-es are flit-ting.

Where the bright blooming flow'rs, Are their o-dors e-mit-ting;

2
Where the saints rob'd in white,
　Cleans'd in life's flowing fountain;
Shining beauteous and bright,
　They inhabit the mountain,
Where no sin nor dismay,
　Neither trouble nor sorrow,
Will be felt for a day,
　Nor be fear'd for the morrow.

3
He's prepared thee a home—
　Sinner, canst thou believe it?
And invites thee to come,
　Sinner, wilt thou receive it?
O come, sinner, come,
　For the tide is receding,
And the Saviour will soon
　And forever cease pleading.

---

98 Angels Hovering Round.

1. There are an-gels hov-'ring round, There are an-gels hov-'ring

round, There are an - - - gels, an - - gels hov-'ring round.

2 To carry the tidings home.
3 To the New Jerusalem.
4 Poor sinners are coming home.

5 And Jesus bids them come.
6 Let him that heareth, come.
7 We are on our journey home.

99. Blessed Assurance.

Words by FANNIE CROSBY. Music by Mrs. JOS. F. KNAPP, by per.

1. Blessed assurance, Jesus is mine! Oh, what a foretaste of glory divine! Heir of salvation, purchased of God, Born of his Spirit, wash'd in his blood.

Chorus.
This is my story, this is my song, Praising my Saviour all the day long; This is my story, this is my song, Praising my Saviour all the day long.

2
Perfect submission, perfect delight,
Visions of rapture burst on my sight;
Angels descending, bring from above,
Echoes of mercy, whispers of love.
Chorus.

3
Perfect submission, all is at rest,
I in my Saviour am happy and blest;
Watching and waiting, looking above,
Fill'd with his goodness, lost in his love.
Chorus.

100. Sweetly Resting.

(Dedicated to Chaplain C. C. McCabe.)

MARY D. JAMES. W. WARREN BENTLEY, by per.

1. In the rift-ed Rock I'm rest-ing, Safe-ly shelter'd I a-bide,
There no foes nor storms mo-lest me, While within the cleft I hide.

Refrain.
Now I'm rest-ing, Sweetly rest-ing, In the cleft once made for me;
Je-sus, bless-ed, Rock of A-ges, I will hide myself in thee.

2
Long pursued by sin and Satan,
Weary, sad, I long'd for rest;
Then I found this heav'nly shelter,
Open'd in my Saviour's breast.
Refrain.—Now I'm resting, &c.

3
Peace, which passeth understanding,
Joy, the world can never give,

Now in Jesus I am finding:
In his smiles of love I live.
Refrain.—Now I'm resting, &c.

4
In the Rifted Rock I'll hide me,
Till the storms of life are past,
All secure in this blest refuge,
Heeding not the fiercest blast.
Refrain.—Now I'm resting, &c.

101. Redeeming Love.

*"Know the love * * * * [in order] that ye might be filled."*—Eph. 3: 19.

J. A. C. Arr. Music by Judge Thos. O. Lowe.

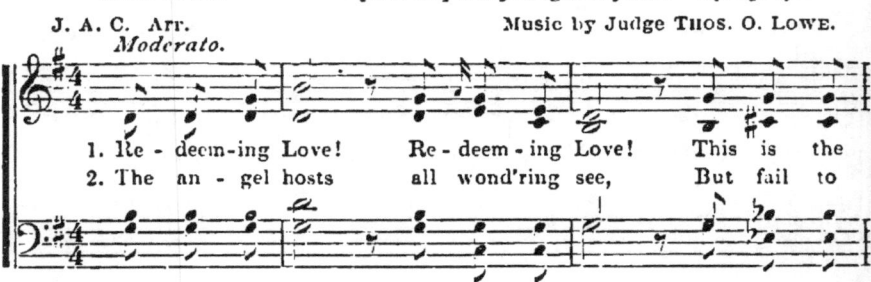

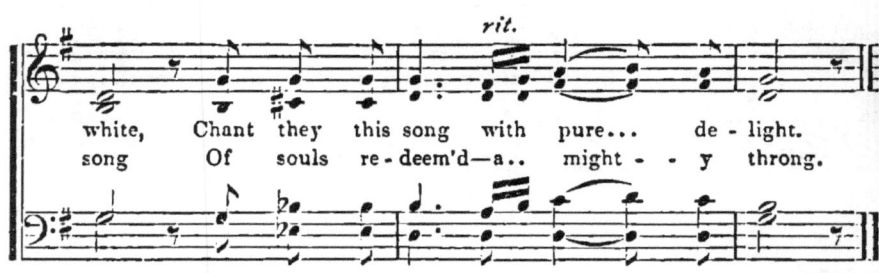

3
And here on earth the pow'r is giv'n
To sing this sweetest song of heav'n;
And our poor voices e'en to raise
In notes of loud and joyous praise.
  Redeeming Love, &c.

4
Oh, shout aloud, ye sons of men!
Tell the glad tidings o'er again:
Oh, earth below! oh, heav'n above,
Sing ye the song—Redeeming Love!
  Redeeming Love, &c.

102. Rest for the Weary.

Words by Rev. S. G. HARMER.   Rev. W. McDONALD.

1. In the Christian's home in glo-ry, There re-mains a land of rest;
There my Saviour's gone be-fore me, To ful-fil my soul's re-quest.

Chorus.

There is rest for the wea-ry, There is rest for the wea-ry, There is rest for the wea-ry, There is rest for you—
On the oth-er side of Jor-dan, In the sweet fields of E-den, Where the tree of life is blooming, There is rest for you.

2
Pain nor sickness ne'er shall enter,
  Grief nor woe my lot shall share;
But in that celestial centre,
  I a crown of life shall wear.
Chorus.—There is rest, &c.

3
Death itself shall then be vanquish'd,
And his sting shall be withdrawn:

Shout for gladness, O ye ransom'd!
  Hail with joy the rising morn.
Chorus.—There is rest, &c.

4
Sing, O sing, ye heirs of glory;
  Shout your triumph as you go;
Zion's gates will open for you,
  You shall find an entrance through.
Chorus.—There is rest, &c.

103. "Let Me Go."

Words and Music by Rev. L. Hartsough.

1. Let me go where saints are going,
To the mansions of the blest;
Let me go where my Redeemer
Has prepar'd his people's rest.
I would gain the realms of brightness,
Where they go out nevermore,
I would join the friends that wait me
Over on the other shore.

2 Let me go where none are weary,
Where is raised no wail of woe;
Let me go, and bathe my spirit
In the raptures angels know:
Let me go, for bliss eternal
Lures my soul away, away,
And the victor's song triumphant,
Thrills my heart, I cannot stay.

3 Let me go, why should I tarry?
What has earth to bind me here?
What, but cares, and toils, and sorrows,
What, but death, and pain and fear?
Let me go, for hopes most cherish'd,
Blasted, round me often lie;
O! I've gathered brightest flowers,
But to see them fade and die.

4 Let me go where tears and sighing
Are forever more unknown;
Where the joyous songs of glory
Call me to a happier home.
Let me go, I'd cease this dying,
I would gain life's fairer plains;
Let me join the myriad harpers,
Let me chant their rapturous strains.

5 Let me go, O speed my journey,
Saints and seraphs lure away;
O! I almost feel the raptures,
That belong to endless day.
Oft methinks I hear the singing
That is only heard above:
Let me go, O speed my going,
Let me go where all is love.

104. Jesus is Mine.

Rev. Horatius Bonar.   T. E. Perkins, by per.

1. Fade, fade each earthly joy, Jesus is mine! Break ev'ry tender tie,
Jesus is mine! Dark is the wilderness, Earth has no resting place,
D.S. Jesus alone can bless, Jesus is mine!

2 Tempt not my soul away,
   Jesus is mine!
Here would I ever stay,
   Jesus is mine!
Perishing things of clay,
Born but for one brief day,
Pass from my heart away,
   Jesus is mine!

3 Farewell, ye dreams of night,
   Jesus is mine!
Lost in this dawning light,
   Jesus is mine!

All that my soul has tried,
   Left but a dismal void,
Jesus has satisfied,
   Jesus is mine!

4 Farewell, mortality,
   Jesus is mine!
Welcome, eternity,
   Jesus is mine!
Welcome, O loved and blest,
Welcome, sweet scenes of rest;
Welcome, my Saviour's breast,
   Jesus is mine!

105. Happy Day.

1. { O happy day that fix'd my choice On thee my Saviour and my God!
    Well may this glowing heart rejoice, And tell its raptures all abroad. }

2
O happy bond, that seals my vows
   To him who merits all my love;
Let cheerful anthems fill his house,
   While to that sacred shrine I move.
Cho.—Happy day, &c.

3
'Tis done, the great transaction's done;
   I am my Lord's, and he is mine;
He drew me, and I follow'd on,
   Charm'd to confess the voice divine.
Cho.—Happy day, &c.

4
Now rest, my long-divided heart,
   Fix'd on this blissful centre, rest;
Nor ever from thy Lord depart:
   With him of every good possess'd.
Cho.—Happy day, &c.

5
High Heav'n, that heard the solemn vow
   That vow renewed shall daily hear,
Till in life's latest hour I bow,
   And bless in death a bond so dear.
Cho.—Happy day, &c.

106. Clinging to the Cross. L. M.

Chorus and Music by Rev. G. C. Wells.

1. When I survey the wondrous cross On which the prince of glory died,
2. Forbid it, Lord, that I should boast, Save in the death of Christ my God;
3. Were the whole realm of nature mine, That were a present far too small;

My richest gain I count but loss, And pour contempt on all my pride.
All the vain things that charm me most, I sacrifice them to his blood.
Love so amazing, so divine, Demands my soul, my life, my all.

Chorus.

{ The cross, the cross, the precious cross, The wondrous cross of Jesus;
{ From all our sin, its guilt and pow'r, And ev-'ry stain it frees us.

Then I'm clinging, clinging, clinging, O, I'm clinging to the cross,
Yes, I'm clinging, clinging, clinging, clinging to the cross.

Copyright, 1869, by JOSEPH HILLMAN.

107. Hallowed Spot.

Words by Rev. W. Hunter, D.D. Arr. for this Work.

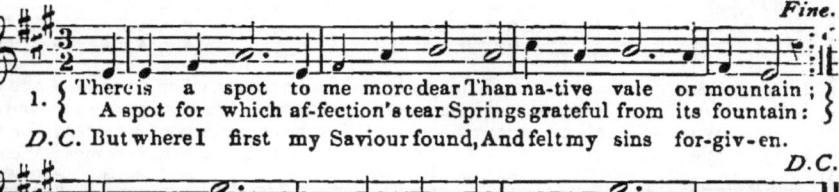

1. There is a spot to me more dear Than native vale or mountain;
A spot for which affection's tear Springs grateful from its fountain:
'Tis not where kindred souls abound, Tho' that on earth is Heaven;
But where I first my Saviour found, And felt my sins forgiven.

2 Hard was my toil to reach the shore,
  Long toss'd upon the ocean;
Above me was the thunder's roar;
  Beneath the waves' commotion:
Darkly the pall of night was thrown
  Around me, faint with terror;
In that dark hour—how did my groan
  Ascend for years of error!

3 Sinking and panting as for breath,
  I knew not help was near me;
And cried, "O! save me, Lord, from death,
  Immortal Jesus, hear me."

Then quick as thought I felt him mine,
  My Saviour stood before me;
I saw his brightness round me shine,
  And shouted "Glory!" "Glory!"

4 Oh, sacred hour! oh, hallow'd spot!
  Where love divine first found me;
Wherever falls my distant lot,
  My heart shall linger round thee;
And when from earth I rise, to soar
  Up to my home in heaven,
Down will I cast my eyes once more,
  Where I was first forgiven.

---

108. Pentecostal Power.

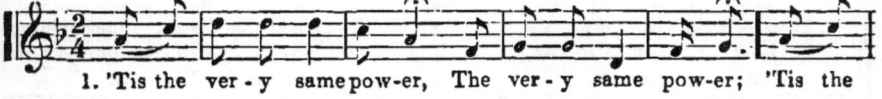

1. 'Tis the very same power, The very same power; 'Tis the very same power That they had at Pentecost; 'Tis the pow'r, the power; 'Tis the pow'r that Jesus promis'd should come down.

2 While with one accord assembled,
  All in an upper room,
Came the power, etc.

3 With cloven tongues of fire,
  And a rushing mighty wind,
Came the power, etc.

4 'Twas while they all were praying,
  And believing it would come,
Came the power, etc.

5 Some thought they were fanatic,
  Or were drunken with new wine;
'Twas the power, etc.

6 Three thousand were converted,
  And were added to the church,
By the power, etc.

7 The martyrs had this power,
  As they triumphed in the flames;
'Twas the power, etc.

8 Our fathers had this power,
  And we may have it too;
'Tis the power, etc.

9 'Tis the very same power,
  For I feel it in my soul;
'Tis the power, etc.

109. Behold the Bridegroom!

Words and Music by (Matt. 25: 6.) R. E. HUDSON.—By per.

1. Are you ready for the Bridegroom When he comes, when he comes? Are you ready for the Bridegroom When he comes, when he comes? Be-hold! he cometh! Be-hold! he com-eth! Be rob'd and ready, for the Bride-groom comes.
2. Have your lamps trimm'd and burning When he comes, when he comes; Have your lamps trimm'd and burning When he comes, when he comes; He quickly cometh, he quick-ly com-eth, O soul! be ready when the Bride-groom comes.
3. We will all go out to meet him When he comes, when he comes; We will all go out to meet him When he comes, when he comes; He surely cometh! he sure-ly com-eth! We'll go to meet him, when the Bride-groom comes.
4. We will chant al-le-lu-ias When he comes, when he comes; We will chant alleluias, When he comes, when he comes; Lo! now he cometh! Lo! now he com-eth! Sing al-le-lu-ia! for the Bride-groom comes.

Chorus.

Behold the Bridegroom, for he comes, for he comes! Behold the Bridegroom, for he comes, for he comes! Behold! he cometh! behold! he cometh! Be rob'd and ready, for the Bridegroom comes!

From "Gems of Gospel Song."

110 Home after Wandering.

Music by Rev. W. McDonald.

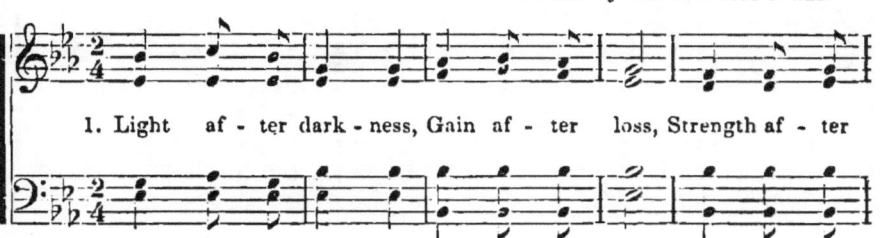

1. Light af-ter dark-ness, Gain af-ter loss, Strength af-ter

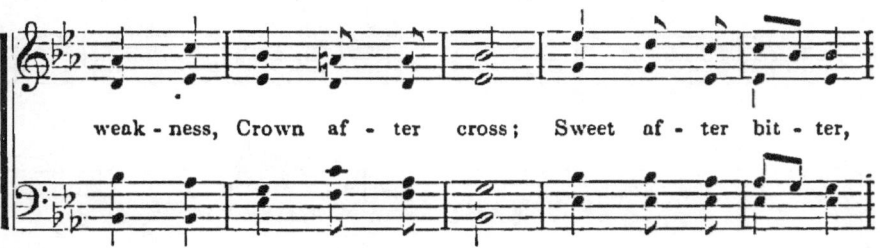

weak-ness, Crown af-ter cross; Sweet af-ter bit-ter,

Song af-ter sigh, Home af-ter wan-der-ing, Praise af-ter cry.

2
Sheaves after sowing,
  Sun after rain,
Sight after mystery,
  Peace after pain,
Joy after sorrow,
  Calm after blast,
Rest after weariness,
  Sweet rest at last.

3
Near after distant,
  Gleam after gloom,
Love after loneliness,
  Life after tomb;
After long agony,
  Rapture of bliss;
Right was the pathway
  Leading to this.

112. Rejoice, His Name is Jesus.

Words and Music by Rev. L. HARTSOUGH.

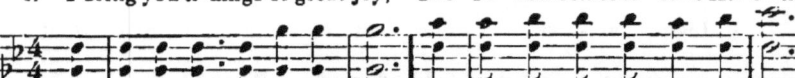
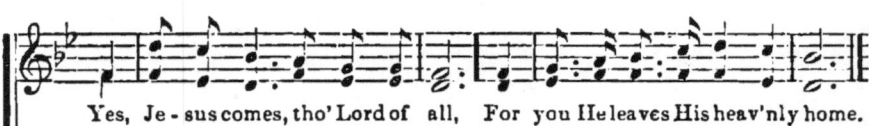
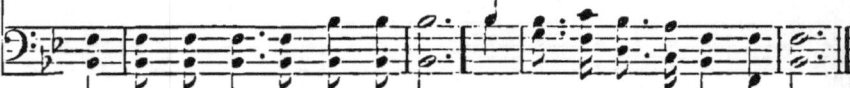
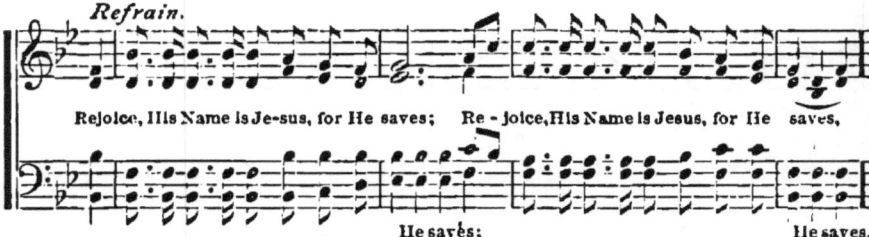

2
Just at the door, with lifted hand,
  He stands and knocks—would enter in;
Who welcomes Christ, with heart and soul,
  Will prove that Jesus saves from sin.
    Refrain.—Rejoice, &c.

3
No other friend can bless as He,
  You've greeted others—welcome Him;
What foes you've had—you thought them friends,
  Jesus, true Friend, will save from sin.
    Refrain.—Rejoice, &c.

4
Besetting sins to Christ will yield,
  Through Him all self will find a grave;
And all this deadly strife will cease,
  As Jesus proves his power to save.
    Refrain.—Rejoice, &c.

5
And Purity is His free gift,
  Thus saving to the uttermost;
And by the Holy Spirit's Power,
  He gives to us our Pentecost.
    Refrain.—Rejoice, &c.

113. "I am the Door."

Har. for this Work. — Words and Melody by Rev. D. WILLIAMS, by per.

1. "I am the door," come in, come in, And leave without thy load of sin; The night is dark, the storm is wild, O venture in, thou stranger child, O, venture in, thou stranger child.

2
"I am the door," come, gently knock,
And I will loose the heavy lock,
That guards my Father's precious fold;
Come in from darkness and from cold.

3
"I am the door," no longer roam,
Here are thy treasures, here thy home;
I purchased them for thee and thine,
And paid the price in blood divine.

4
"I am the door," my Father waits
To make thee heir of rich estates;
Come, dwell with him, and dwell with me,
And thou my Father's child shall be.

5
"I am the door," come in, come in,
And everlasting treasures win;
My Father's house was built for thee,
And thou shalt share his home with me.

114. America.

Words by Rev. S. F. SMITH.

1
My faith looks up to thee,
Thou Lamb of Calvary,
  Saviour divine,
Now hear me while I pray:
Take all my guilt away;
O let me from this day
  Be wholly thine.

2
May thy rich grace impart
Strength to my fainting heart;
  My zeal inspire;
As thou hast died for me,
O may my love to thee
Pure, warm and changeless be,
  A living fire.

3
While life's dark maze I tread,
And griefs around me spread,
  Be thou my guide;
Bid darkness turn to day;
Wipe sorrow's tears away,
Nor let me ever stray
  From thee aside.

115 Cross and Crown. C. M.

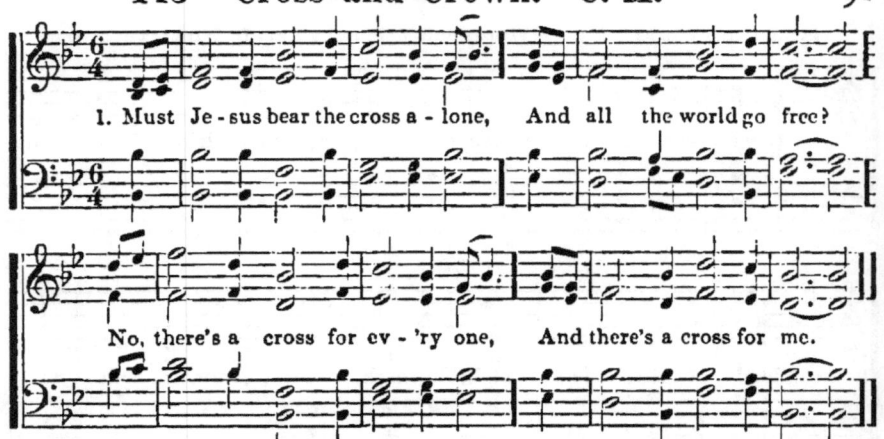

1. Must Jesus bear the cross alone, And all the world go free? No, there's a cross for ev-'ry one, And there's a cross for me.

2 How happy are the saints above
Who once went sorrowing here;
But now they taste unmingled love,
And joy without a tear.

3 The consecrated cross I'll bear
Till death shall set me free,
And then go home my crown to wear,
For there's a crown for me.

4 Upon the crystal pavement, down
At Jesus' pierced feet,
Joyful, I'll cast my golden crown,
And his dear name repeat.

5 O precious cross! O glorious crown!
O resurrection day!
Ye angels, from the stars come down,
And bear my soul away.

116

1 Lord, I believe a rest remains
To all thy people known;
A rest where pure enjoyment reigns,
And thou art loved alone:

2 A rest, where all our soul's desire
Is fix'd on things above;
Where fear, and sin, and grief expire,
Cast out by perfect love.

3 O that I now the rest might know,
Believe, and enter in:
Now, Saviour, now the power bestow,
And make me free from sin.

4 To me the rest of faith impart,
The Sabbath of thy love;
Give me the new and perfect heart
That Satan cannot move.

117

1 O for a heart to praise my God,
A heart from sin set free: —
A heart that always feels thy blood,
So freely spilt for me!

2 A heart resign'd, submissive, meek,
My great Redeemer's throne;
Where only Christ is heard to speak,—
Where Jesus reigns alone.

3 O for a lowly, contrite heart,
Believing, true, and clean;
Which neither life nor death can part
From him that dwells within:—

4 A heart in every thought renew'd,
And full of love Divine;
Perfect, and right, and pure, and good,
A copy, Lord, of thine.

118

1 Come, O my God, the promise seal,
This mountain sin remove:
Now, in my waiting soul reveal
The virtue of thy love.

2 I want thy life, thy purity,
Thy righteousness brought in;
I ask, desire, and trust in thee,
To be redeemed from sin.

3 Saviour, to thee my soul looks up,
My present Saviour thou!
In all the confidence of hope,
I claim the blessing now.

4 'Tis done: thou dost this moment save,
With full salvation bless;
Redemption through thy blood I have,
And spotless love and peace,

119 Let Nothing Divide Us.

Words and Music by Rev. L. HARTSOUGH.

2 As the branch to the Vine is united,
　　And knows but the life it will gain,
　So would I be joined to Thee—Jesus
　　Now take me, and set up Thy reign.—*Refrain.*

3 The chill of this world, like the frost-work
　　That vanishes fast from the Sun,
　Must yield to Thy life-giving presence:
　　For Thou art now claiming Thine own.—*Refrain.*

4 Who'll sever the nuptials completed,
　　Whilst Thou art my Keeper and Love?
　What princes or powers can harm me,
　　Whilst in Thee, and by Thee I move?—*Refrain.*

5 Oh, bring out Thine Image in beauty
　　Upon my whole being within;
　And may I in walk and in duty
　　Reveal Thee, my Saviour from sin.—*Refrain.*

120. The Pilgrim Company.

Arranged by Rev. W. McDonald.

1. What poor despised company
Of travelers are these,
Who walk in yonder narrow way,
Along that rugged maze?

Cho.—I had rather be the least of them,
Who are the Lord's alone,
Than wear a royal diadem,
And sit upon a throne.
And sit upon a throne, And sit upon a throne;
Than wear a royal diadem, And sit upon a throne.

2 Ah! these are of a royal line,
All children of a King,
Heirs of immortal crowns divine,
And lo! for joy they sing.

3 Why do they then appear so mean?
And why so much despised?
Because of their rich robes unseen
The world is not apprised.

4 But some of them seem poor, distressed,
And lacking daily bread;
Ah! they're of boundless wealth possess'd
With heavenly manna fed.

5 Why do they shun the pleasing path
That worldlings love so well?
Because it is the way to death,
The open road to hell.

6 But why keep they the narrow road,
That rugged thorny maze?
Why that's the way their leader trod,
They love and keep his ways.

7 What, is there then no other road
To Salem's happy ground?
Christ is the only way to God,
None other can be found.

121 What a Friend we have in Jesus.

"There is a Friend that sticketh closer than a Brother."—Prov. 18: 24.

HORATIUS BONAR, D. D. CHARLES C. CONVERSE, 1868, by per.

2
Have we trials and temptations?
 Is there trouble anywhere?
We should never be discouraged,
 Take it to the Lord in prayer.
Can we find a Friend so faithful,
 Who will all our sorrows share?
Jesus knows our every weakness,
 Take it to the Lord in prayer.

3
Are we weak and heavy-laden,
 Cumbered with a load of care?
Precious Saviour, still our refuge,—
 Take it to the Lord in prayer.
Do thy friends despise, forsake thee?
 Take it to the Lord in prayer;
In his arms he'll take and shield thee,
 Thou wilt find a solace there.

INDEX OF TUNES.

Title	Page	Title	Page
A home over there	75	I will not let Thee go	40
Adoration	65	Jesus, my joy	21
And can it be	53	Jesus calls me	32
Angels hovering round	78	Jesus paid it all	47
Are you washed in the Blood	30	Jesus is mine	84
Azmon	59	Let me go	83
America	90	Lights along the shore	50
Balerma	59	Let nothing divide us	92
Behold the Bridegroom	87	More like Thee	51
Beulah Land	12	My heart song	56
Blessed assurance	79	Nothing but the blood of Jesus	48
Bringing in the sheaves	3	Northfield	57
Child, your Father calls	17	Oh, sing of His mighty love	34
Christ received by faith	57	Only in the name of Jesus	76
Close to Thee	11	Our loved ones in Heaven	73
Cleansing Fountain	13	Pentecostal Power	86
Clinging to the cross	85	Redeeming Love	81
Cleanse me, O Lord	70	Remembered by what I have done	52
Come to Jesus	23	Rest for the weary	82
Consecration	10	Rejoice, and be glad	14
Companionship with Jesus	18	Rock of Ages	60
Coronation	59	Royal way of the Cross	60
Deliverance will come	8	Rejoice, his Name is Jesus	89
Dennis	45	Skeptic, spare that Book	54
Die on the field of battle	87	Streaming Mercy	51
Entire Consecration	29	Sweetly Resting	80
Free	38	Take me as I am	22
Full Salvation	26	The child of a King	69
Glory to the Lamb	48	Tell it to Jesus alone	67
Glory to His Name	77	The Cleansing Wave	6
Hallelujah, Jesus saves	74	The Cross	49
Hallowed Spot	86	The half was never told	35
Happy Day	84	The Precious Blood	43
Heart Longings	63	The Open Gate	72
Heavenly Home	68	The sinner invited	78
Home after wandering	88	The valley of Blessing	58
Home beyond the tide	55	The Pilgrim Company	93
How can I keep from singing	31	The Stranger at the Door	41
I am glad there is cleansing	15	Waiting at the Pool	66
I am the Door	90	White as snow	16
I am trusting, Lord, in Thee	5	Whiter than snow	20
I hear Thy welcome voice	4	Whosoever Believeth	71
I cling, dear Lord, to Thee	19	Who'll stand up for Jesus	9
I'm Redeemed	24	We'll bear the Cross	62
I love to tell the story	37	Wonderous Love	27
In the morning	39	Work for Jesus	33
I rest upon His promise	25	Wrestling Jacob	44
Is your lamp burning, my brother	46	What a Friend we have in Jesus	94
I've been Redeemed	64	Why not to-night	42
I will follow Thee	36		

INDEX TO NUMBERS.

Title	Nos.
And can it be that I	65
And can my heart aspire	9
And can I yet delay	56
A charge to keep I have	55
Amid the hours that	87
All hail the power	74
Ah, many years	22
Are you ready for the Bridegroom	109
Are you weary	86
Away, my unbelieving fear	66
Because for me	8
Behold a Stranger	48
Blessed assurance	99
Close to Thee	15
Come home, dear sinner	23
Come, every soul	29
Come, O my God, the promise	118
Come, O thou traveller	51
Come, my fond, fluttering heart	70
Come all ye saints	92
Come let us use the grace	76
Create in me, Lord	89
Dear Jesus, I long	26
Down at the Cross	96
Down in the valley	84
Drooping souls	80
Father, I dare believe	53
Father, Son, and Holy Ghost	79
Forever here my rest shall be	28
Fountain of life	7
From Calvary's mountain	90
Fade, fade each earthly joy	104
Firmly, brethren	109
God loved the world	34
Have you been to Jesus	37
How bright the hope	2
I am coming to the Cross	3
I bring you tidings of great joy	112
I would be Thine	10
I saw a way-worn traveller	12
I've reached the land of corn and	16
I hear Thy welcome voice	21
I cling, dear Lord, to Thee	25
I've found a joy in sorrow	27
I will follow Thee, my Saviour	43
I love to tell the story	44
I hear the Saviour say thy strength	58
I have entered the valley of blessing	73
I do not want one thought	82
I know I love Thee better, Lord	42
I know that my Redeemer lives	71
In the morning of the waking	46
In the rifted Rock	100
In the Christian's home	102
I'm a pilgrim and a stranger	62
I am the Door	113
Jesus, lover of my soul	4
Jesus, my Lord, to Thee I cry	28
Jesus, to Thee I now can fly	11
Jesus hath died that I might live	75
Jesus calls me, I am going	39
Jesus, Lord, I come to Thee	31
Jesus, Saviour, great example	63
Jesus, united by Thy grace	72
Just as I am	28
Let Him to whom we now belong	30
Let me go, the day is breaking	47
Let me go where saints are going	103
Let nothing divide us, dear Saviour	92
Light after darkness	110
Lord, I believe a rest remains	32–116
Many at the Cross are kneeling	93
Many years of bondage	45
Must Jesus bear the Cross alone	115
My body, soul and spirit	14
My faith looks up to Thee	114
My Father is rich in houses and lands	88
My God, my God, to Thee I cry	6
My life flows on in endless song	38
No love to give, no tears to weep	81
O, bliss of the purified	41
O, blessed fellowship divine	24
O, come and dwell in me	54
O, do not let the Word depart	49
O, for a heart to praise my God	117
O, happy day, that fixed my choice	105
O, now I see the crimson wave	5
O, think of a home over there	94
O, skeptic, spare that Book	67
O, who'll stand up for Jesus	13
Precious Saviour, thou hast saved	33
Redeeming Love	101
Rejoice and be glad	19
Rock of Ages, cleft for me	78
Sad and weary with my longing	61
Say, is your lamp burning	57
Sinner go, will you go	97
Sowing in the morning	1
Take my life, and let it be	36
The cross, the cross, the blood	50
There is a fountain fill'd with blood	17–83
There is a gate stands open wide	91
There is peace only in His name	95
There are angels hovering round	98
There is a spot to me more dear	107
The world is overcome by the blood	60
The great Physician now is near	35
Thousands stand to-day in sorrow	85
'Tis the very same power	108
Up and away, like the dew	64
We praise thee, O God! for the Son	20
We have toiled in many vineyards	40
We are out on the ocean sailing	68
We may spread our couch with roses	77
What can wash away my sin?	59
What a Friend we have in Jesus	121
When I survey the wondrous Cross	106
What poor despised company	120
Yield to me now, for I am weak	52

www.ingramcontent.com/pod-product-compliance
Lightning Source LLC
Chambersburg PA
CBHW020901160426
43192CB00007B/1022